FAMILY REDEFINED:

CHILDHOOD REFLECTIONS ON THE IMPACT OF DIVORCE

KIMBERLY EWERTZ

LITTLE CREEK PRESS®
AND BOOK DESIGN
MINERAL POINT, WISCONSIN

Little Creek Press®
A Division of Kristin Mitchell Design, Inc.
5341 Sunny Ridge Road
Mineral Point, Wisconsin 53565

Book Design and Project Coordination:
Little Creek Press and Book Design

Cover design: Anthony Scotino

First Printing
October 2020

Printed in Wisconsin, United States of America

For more information or to order books,
email: familyredefinedthebook@gmail.com,
www.familyredefinedbook.com,
or visit: www.littlecreekpress.com

Library of Congress Control Number: 2020917830

ISBN-13: 978-1-942586-88-3

Dedication

To my son, Tony, I offer this book in lieu of the answers
and honesty you needed when your life turned upside down.
My love for you knows no bounds.

Praise for Family Redefined: Childhood Reflections on the Impact of Divorce

Family Redefined: Childhood Reflections on the Impact of Divorce offers readers an in-depth exploration of divorce. Ten adults, each with a unique story and family dynamic, tell their personal accounts of divorce from their own life.

Told with honesty and candor, often painful and overwhelming, we step into their shoes as they navigate the changes divorce brings to their daily life, their family, and their journey to adulthood.

Each chapter concludes with the author's thoughts of her own journey of divorce with her child, and offers the wisdom that parents and children can, "emerge from these trials and tribulations all the stronger."

An excellent conversation starter this book can facilitate complex and interesting discussions about the emotions and changes divorce brings. For parents and support groups this book offers validation that you are not alone and a heartfelt hope that families can heal through open and honest discussion.

~Sharon Kelly, Librarian

Each short story provides an opportunity for the reader to relate personally to their divorce experience, and to have a sense of validation. Practical insight is also offered for those going through divorce, and their loved ones. Ewertz shares her deep honest thoughts, where she offers the opportunity for someone else to find healing that she has found herself.

~Christine Morris,
Marriage and Family Therapist Associate #116780,
Discovery Counseling Center

Ewertz truly captures Ellen's story of emotional turmoil as she adjusted to her parents' divorce. Her story is a prime example of the subsequent life-long changes that result when there is not stability in the home and the psychological impact this causes to children that often continues into adulthood.

~Betsy Becker, Writer/Motivational Blogger

The chapter, Katniss, captures the essence of the turmoil facing children of divorce, as well as the long-lasting effects that they endure even years later. Ewertz parallels perfectly her own divorce experience to help the reader understand the true depth of the pain caused by divorce, as well as the importance of communication and unconditional love throughout the healing process.

~Luke Niedringhaus

Family Redefined is a helpful resource to divorcing parents as they seek to support their children. Most parents worry about the effect of their decision on their children's welfare. Ewertz approaches this very sensitive subject with compassionate insight from her own experiences, as well as professional guidance from therapists.

Ewertz tells the real life stories of individuals who are children of divorce, sharing their thoughts and feelings, both past and present. Weaving in the comments of therapists brings insight to the effect of parent choices and guidance in how to nurture health for these families who are redefined by these changes.

I particularly appreciated her reflections on her own divorce in each chapter. She realized the dynamics of divorce were much more complicated for her son than she knew or understood. *Family Redefined* is her gift of insight and guidance to those who are currently in the midst of it as a help along the way.

~Vicki Minerva, LMFT, www.vickiminerva.com

This book captures the painful but important, often untold stories of children and their experiences of divorce. Ewertz offers additional talking points for parents who are aiming to reduce the negative impact of divorce on their children. A must read for both adults of childhood divorce and for parents embarking on this challenging life course.

~Linnea Terranova, Psy. D. Founder and Clinical psychologist, Wellspring Psychological Services, Inc.

Ewertz has written a wise and wildly insightful book about divorce and its effects on the lives of those involved—the parents and especially the children.

~Seth Harwood, bestselling author of *In Broad Daylight, Jack Wakes Up,* and *The Maltese Jordans*

Ewertz writes with confident self-awareness as she injects her research and personal reflections into each story featured in *Family Redefined.* She relays the painful and triumphant experiences of children of divorce with care, dignity, and insight. *Family Redefined*will be a useful tool for those on a path toward healing the wounds of divorce.

~Anne Bigley Chand, MLIS

Ewertz has the ability to transport the reader into the personal story and pain of the men and women that were brave enough to share their stories. As the Local Mission Director, at a church, I plan to keep a handful of these books on my bookshelf so I may hand them out to folks that come in looking for support from the pain of going through divorce, or an adult seeking solace from childhood hurts.

~Tammy Stone, Mission Director, South Valley Community Church

Table of Contents

Acknowledgments

This book would not be possible without the consent and participation of the brave and selfless individuals who willingly shared their time and the story of their lives in hope that children and parents everywhere would benefit from their testimonies. I will forever owe them a lifetime of gratitude.

I wish to thank my editors and proofreaders, Carly Gelsinger, and Jordan Rosenfeld, who provided their professional skills and talents in addition to their personal feedback. I give thanks as well to Seth Harwood, someone I consider my mentor, teacher, and advisor who assisted me in my writing career as well as my journey to create this book. My eternal appreciation goes to my publisher, Kristin Mitchell, owner of Little Creek Press and Book Design, (LCP), who worked with me every step of the way. You made my dream come true, Kristin. I also want to thank as well all those associated with LCP, who worked alongside Kristin to ensure the book's completion.

I am grateful for the support and enthusiasm of my dear friends who accompanied me throughout my journey to complete this book. So, to Betsy Becker Niedringhaus, my adopted sister, I thank you from the bottom of my heart for your continuous encouragement all along the way. To Maureen Pramanik, good friend and faithful supporter, I offer you my thanks. My thanks as well to Sandy Gorham Salger, Tammy Stone, Rosie Grimm, Kathy MacPhail, Paula Olsen, and Teresa Stephenson for their support and belief in this book. To librarian Sharon Kelly, who confirmed my belief there was most definitely a need for this book, I offer my thanks. Special thanks to Dr. David Royko, author of the book Voices of Children of Divorce, published in 2000, who was gracious enough to grant me an interview and provide invaluable insight into the world of children of divorce.

The ability to dedicate four years of my life in researching and writing this book could not have been possible without the support and love of my husband, Steven. His confidence in me and my endeavor never wavered, even when I doubted myself. He provided me the will to continue and complete my goal. Thank you, my love, from the bottom of my heart. Our introduction to one another, which took place over thirty years ago, was the start of the best years of my life.

There is one more individual who deserves my unending thanks and has my unconditional love—my son, Tony. His steadfast devotion and belief in my ability to write this book was the ongoing motivation behind every page. His cover design brought to life the meaning I hoped to convey within the pages of this book. The exuberance and affirmation he provided me from the first mention of this book have never faltered. Knowing that it has helped him means the world to me. ❤

Author's Note

F*amily Redefined: Childhood Reflections on the Impact of Divorce* is a work of creative nonfiction. Within the pages of this book are testimonials depicted by selfless individuals who agreed to share the intimate details of their lives in the hope it would help others. All the names and identifying details of these individuals have been changed to protect their privacy as well as the privacy of their families and loved ones. ❤

Introduction

If not for my naivete, this book may never have been written. After twelve years of marriage living in a toxic environment, I filed for divorce, certain that I was making the right choice for my son and myself. I never expected this decision to catapult my son into a world of confusion and chaos and was certainly ill-equipped to handle it.

My son was ten years old at the time, and I believed there couldn't be any negative repercussions because I was removing us from a volatile and abusive situation. I soon found out how wrong my presumption was. My son's anger became apparent soon after his father moved out. It manifested in a number of small yet subtle ways: refusing to go to school, keeping me at a distance, and at times erupting into bursts of anger over minor disagreements—a complete departure from the congenial and happy child he'd always been.

His most devastating reaction was aimed directly at me. Our bedtime routine was one I'd cherished. I'd tuck him in, read him a bed time story, gently kiss his forehead, and whisper, "I love you."

By the time I reached his door, I'd be gifted with his customary response, "I love you too, Mom."

After the divorce, our routine changed. I still tucked him in, I still read him a bedtime story, and I still wished him a good night, but instead of his nightly, "I love you's," his response was silence. The first time he failed to respond, my heart felt as though it stopped. When it happened the following night, and the night after that, and the night after that, I convinced myself he was going through a phase. That phase lasted nine months. When he finally spoke the words I'd longed to hear, "I love you, Mom." I bolted across the room, grabbed him, and held him in my arms, never wanting to let go. My little boy was back!

Adults rarely consider how divorce is interpreted by a child, which is why I felt this book was not only necessary but vital for divorced parents, offering them a child's insight of the impact this life-altering decision has on them. The personal stories shared within these pages offer parents an opportunity to travel the rocky path of divorce from a child's viewpoint—a child who not only traveled it but came out the other side.

The brave men and women featured in this book have shared their experiences, both good and bad. These testaments to those currently enmeshed in the perils of divorce offer hope that there will come a day when you and your child will return to a place of normalcy, though it may be a new definition of normalcy.

For those currently traveling this uncharted journey of uncertainty that follows divorce, the question continues to linger: Did I make the right decision? As certain as you may be that you did, the haunting mantra of "what if?" remains. I know it did for me. It is moments like my son's long overdue "I love you" that feed a parent's hope to hold on. Things will work out. Your story will have a happy ending. For a parent going through this difficult journey, waiting for those moments acknowledging that you've made the right choice is nothing short of agonizing.

But as you continue along your path, never forget that your child is right there with you every step of the way, and he or she is experiencing the same angst, fear, and confusion as you. But in addition to those revolving emotions, they are also trying to comprehend what has happened to their family. Why has their world been turned upside down? This is a crucial time. A parent's guidance, support, and above all, unconditional love is needed more now than ever.

It is my sincere hope that this book offers all who read it the message: you are not alone. I ask that you hold onto that fact. I ask that you hold onto your child. I ask that you hold onto the belief that it will get better, because it will. My son and I are living proof of that. ❤

CHAPTER ONE

LISA

Lisa, an only child, was six years old when her parents separated. Now fifty-six, Lisa vividly recalls the day her parents informed her of their decision, which ultimately changed the course of her life. The memory of that day still ignites a sense of anxiety and insecurity, traits of Lisa's personality that she carried with her into adulthood.

❤

The Announcement

The six-year-old, dressed in blue jeans and a faded T-shirt, her Keds scuffed at the toes, sat on the couch and watched in silence. Her parents, who appeared to be moving in slow motion, turned their backs to her and entered their bedroom. Lisa watched her father's hand turn the doorknob, and then she heard the metallic click of the lock.

Lisa was met with a surprise when she had arrived home that day. Katie, her mother—who normally worked during the day—was waiting for her when she came through the front door. In stoic silence, Katie motioned for Lisa to take a seat on the couch. The little girl watched her mom wipe tears from her face as Katie explained in a quivering voice that she and her father needed to talk, and afterward, they would want to talk to Lisa.

"Until then, wait quietly like a good girl," Katie instructed.

Living in a stressful environment had become the norm for Lisa. Her parents had married young. Katie was eighteen at the time and six months pregnant with Lisa. Stan, Lisa's father, was nineteen. Stan's habitual criticizing not only of Katie but also of Lisa led the child to develop an eating disorder very early on, overeating in times of stress as a type of self-punishment for not meeting her father's standards.

Lisa sat on the edge of the dark brown couch, feeling the ridges of the corduroy material between her fingers, half-watching Mr. Rogers Neighborhood. She couldn't focus. Her stomach felt just like it did when she'd accidentally swallowed a peach pit. She bit down on her lower lip as she stared at the locked door, waiting for it to open. After what felt like hours, Lisa decided she'd had enough waiting.

She stood up and marched to the door, hesitating a beat before rapping her knuckles against it.

"We'll be out soon," Katie called.

Lisa's heart jumped at the sound of her mother's voice, which sounded muffled and hoarse. She returned to the couch, and a few minutes later, her parents joined her in the living room. Her mother sat beside her, and her father chose the oversized chair across the room from them both.

"Your dad's going to go away for a while," Katie explained. "He'll still be around, but he just won't be with us anymore."

Lisa looked from her mother and then to her father, who was avoiding her eyes.

"Okay, let's eat something," Lisa said.

Nearly five decades later, sitting on her couch in her two-bedroom apartment, Lisa recalls that day with clarity and regret.

"The moment that came out of my mouth, I felt like crap. I said it like that, in front of my dad. And then I had angst over that, and guilt, like crazy. I felt like, oh, now my dad thinks I don't care for him," she says.

Lisa vehemently shakes her head, her short hair tossing side to side, trying to dismiss the memory from her mind, but the pain in her pale blue eyes indicates that's not possible. The sting of guilt is a powerful injury.

The New Normal

Soon after the announcement, Lisa and her mother moved out of the family home, and Stan moved in with his parents, never debating Katie's insistence she assume full custody of their child.

Living full-time with her mother ignited an overprotective obsession in Lisa regarding her welfare. If she noticed Katie was feeling down, Lisa felt it was her responsibility to cheer her up. Fortunately, Katie handled these scenarios with affirmation and reassured Lisa time and again that the separation wasn't her fault.

"She would say to me, 'Lisa, this has nothing to do with you. It's something I have to figure out, and I'm going to, and everything is going to be fine,'" Lisa says.

Lisa releases a heavy sigh as she reflects on those early days. Her biggest regret is that her mother felt the necessity to put on a happy face, hiding the fears and insecurities she felt, always wanting to appear strong for Lisa's sake.

"If my mom would have said, 'You know, Lisa, I want to do the best by you, and for you, but I'm feeling like I'm failing.' Or, 'I'm not doing enough for you,' that would have helped," Lisa says. "Because it's great to be the strong one for your kid, but if your kid is probably going through the same emotions, you could get a lot of camaraderie from that. It's like, you know what, let's band together and see what we can do and figure it out together."

Marriage and Family Therapist Vicki Minerva agrees that an honest relationship between parent and child is beneficial, but the key is *how* the parent communicates that truth to the child.

"I would communicate that you've got support. You've got friends, you've got family, you've got classes you can take. You can say, 'I'm learning how to take care of myself so I can take care of us.' A child needs to know an adult has resources. Those are important things. When that's not true, it's a scarier situation. And you don't want to have the child become parentified and feeling like they have to take care of the parent."

Abandonment Issues

Even though Lisa spent a great deal of her after-school time with her grandparents, Stan's parents, their son was rarely home, which Lisa believes was a conscious effort on her father's part. Times with her father were infrequent, at best.

Lisa's relationship with her father had always been somewhat strained, even before the separation, but after, Stan's absences had a greater impact on the six-year-old. Lisa would find herself thinking about him and wondering if he was missing her.

"I would idolize him because of not seeing him too much," Lisa says.

As Stan pulled away from Lisa, Katie realized the effect his absence was having on her daughter.

"So, my mom I guess called him and said, 'Hey, you need to spend some time with your kid.'"

Katie had another motive as well: finding time for herself. "My mom didn't get to do anything. When she wasn't working, she was being a parent," Lisa says.

Katie's prodding resulted in Stan accompanying Lisa to a number of her favorite places, including the Ice Capades and dog shows, but it was never just the two of them. On each of the outings, Stan invited at least one of Lisa's friends to tag along, leaving Lisa to believe he never wanted to spend time together with just her.

Lisa's insecurity was compounded by his habitual belittlement. He compared her to the other children and asked why she couldn't be more like them. This additional emotional stress resulted in Lisa becoming comfortable with self-abuse.

"I just hid myself in food," she says. "That was the only way I could get some gratification or satisfaction."

One particular incident—when Stan invited Lisa and her friend to go to the zoo—still stands out as a low point in their relationship. Sitting in the back seat of her father's Lincoln Town Car, Lisa and her best friend, Jill, played *I Spy* as Stan navigated the highway. The girls, excited about their outing, called out familiar landmarks along the way.

"There's the McDonald's where I had my birthday party," Lisa said with a smile that showed the gap between her two front teeth.

But the fun was spoiled almost as soon as they arrived at the zoo. The gift shop was their first stop.

"How about I buy each of you a T-shirt. Would you like that?" Stan said.

The girls immediately responded, shouting, "Yes!" in unison.

Stan smiled and then added, "But, you have to let me pick out the shirts."

The girls entertained themselves with animal figurines as Stan browsed through the racks of T-shirts. Caught up in their play, they almost missed when Stan called to them that he was ready to leave. Carefully, the girls placed the miniature statues back on the shelves and then headed out the door to meet up with Stan, who was waiting for them with a large bag in his hand.

Reaching into the bag, he ceremoniously pulled out a pale pink T-shirt with a picture of a princess on the front. Lisa went for the shirt, but Stan pulled it out of her reach.

"This one's for Jill because she's such a little princess. I hope you like it," Stan said, handing Jill the shirt as she squealed with delight.

Lisa made an unsuccessful attempt to peek inside the bag.

"Patience, Lisa, patience," he said with a smile. Only his smile reminded Lisa of the villain in a Disney movie.

Lisa waited as her father reached inside the bag and pulled out a purple and red shirt featuring a giant human mouth on the front. In big, bold letters it read, DO NOT FEED. Lisa's smile fell, her face reddened, and her throat grew tight. Jill quickly hid her new shirt behind her back.

"I don't want it," Lisa said, just before turning her back on her father.

Lisa's face reddens once again as she recalls the anger that consumed her that day.

"I was pissed. I was pissed at the stupid place for even having a shirt like that. I'll never forget it," she says.

Over the next few years, Lisa began to see through her father's bravado. "You couldn't count on one thing that man said. He would say anything that made himself look good, and others look bad. He always had to be the big guy," Lisa says.

But he was still her father. Lisa's longing for his love and acceptance continually led to disappointment and heart-ache throughout her childhood.

A Child's Need to Connect

As with many parents, Katie had precious little time to unwind and relax. The stress of juggling a full-time job, maintaining a home, and caring for her child exhausted her, even with her in-laws stepping in to get Lisa to and from school each day and hosting weekly dinners. But as much as Lisa loved her grandparents, she truly looked forward to having one-on-one time with her mother.

"I'm like bouncing off the walls to see her, and we get home, and mom is just exhausted. She wants to just come home, make dinner, and read a good book while I watch TV," Lisa says.

Unfortunately, Lisa interpreted Katie's exhaustion as ambivalence, feeling as though her mother didn't enjoy being in her company.

Lisa's desire to connect with her mother exemplifies the unconscious need that children of divorce typically experience—the need for physical interaction with the parent.

Licensed Marriage and Family Therapist Pete Collom suggests that parents use what he calls kinesthetic work, or tactile learning, during this time. This type of therapy is especially helpful for young children dealing with trauma, initiating games like wrestling or rough-and-tumble play, which provide physical interaction with the child and the parent.

"Kids work through their issues through play. They don't do it verbally; they do it physically. You have to work with the body. The body is not just remembering visual or auditory or verbal; it's a memory physically of everything that they're experiencing. And that anger and that pain live in their body," Collom says.

Often, children transitioning through their parents' separation or divorce display personality changes and behaviors as a result of the trauma they are experiencing. Collom explains, "Most of the time, a child starts to act out, which is normal for crises and divorce. They regress, extroverts become introverts and introverts become more extroverted. Those are signs that they are under a lot of anxiety, a lot of stress. That's when parents tend to not deal with it very effectively. They become more critical, they punish more, they take things away, and they forget that what the child is really asking for is some kind of connection."

During the difficult transition of divorce or separation, Collom strongly urges parents to spend quality one-on-one time with their child. "Really focus on the child. Don't let other outside activities come in," he says.

Collom feels it's equally important to do what the *child* wants to do during that one-on-one time, as it offers them a true sense of connectedness.

Dating and New Partners

A parent's decision to date is another aspect of divorce that can affect the child. This definitely was true for Lisa due to her irrational fear of abandonment resulting from her father's departure from her life after the separation.

"The dating thing was hard. All of a sudden, some guy would show up, and they were dating or something. The guys were nice, but it was just that my mom was paying attention to someone other than me," Lisa says. "I was always scared that something was going to happen to her, and I'd be alone. I think I was just afraid that my mom was going to ditch me. My dad ditched me."

As much as Lisa disliked the idea of her mother going out, she became angry with herself and plagued with guilt if Katie chose to stay home with her.

"I kind of felt bad for my mom," Lisa says with a sigh. "How was she going to find somebody with me around?"

When parents begin dating, the fear children experience is associated with the common fantasy that their parents will one day reunite. In Lisa's case, her parents maintained a lengthy separation, several years before divorcing, which only added to her expectations. The importance associated with this fantasy hinges on the fact that a child's identity is tied directly to his or her family. When the family falls apart, the child's sense of self becomes threatened and leads to identity confusion.

In Katie's case, she did find someone Lisa accepted and liked. His name was Bill. As a father to a young son, Bill was able to relate to Lisa in a parental way. It's not surprising that Lisa accepted Bill into her life, considering her need for a stable male role model. Bill provided just that.

When it comes to the introduction of a new partner, Minerva suggests waiting a while before introducing this person to the children. "Until you know that it is something that has a future expectation."

When the relationship moves beyond dating, the subject of disciplinary roles comes into play. Minerva recommends that role continue to be carried out by the original parent, not the stepparent.

"Especially as the relationship is forming, I would say the older the child is, the more critical that becomes. A teenager is not going to respond as well to a stepparent telling them what to do. But there should be an agreement between the couple as to what the rules are," Minerva says.

Soon after the separation, Stan started attending church, and through his newfound faith, he also found love with a woman named Pam, a member of his new congregation. Two years after the separation, he and Pam married.

Stan's decision to marry prompted a legal divorce, which allowed Katie to move forward with her life. Once the divorce was finalized, Bill and Katie married and moved the family to a new home.

Adjusting to a New Home

As positive as the move was for Lisa, she found herself battling bouts of anxiety brought on by her new surroundings. Lisa wistfully stares out her living room window as she recalls how much she missed the scent of eucalyptus trees in the backyard of her old house. Throughout this adjustment period, Lisa was plagued with countless sleepless nights. Being a resourceful child, she discovered her own method of calming herself down at bedtime.

Lisa's new room, adorned with toys, posters, and books also included her very own record player in addition to a small collection of albums. One of her favorites in that collection was the comedy album by Bill Cosby.

Each night at bedtime, Lisa would remove the album from its sleeve, then gently place the needle onto the first groove of the album. Once the needle was in place, Lisa would scurry across the room and then jump into bed, pull the covers up all around her, lean back against her headboard, and revel in the comedian's stories of his childhood days.

"It would just be on repeat all night. He was really good at describing his childhood. He had friends and all this going on and I didn't have all that. And his parents were always there," Lisa says.

Katie, who was very perceptive of her daughter's needs, realized that Lisa was struggling with the move and decided to do something about it. First, she hand-painted Lisa's book shelves in her favorite colors, and then the two went on a shopping trip.

"I got Snoopy sheets, and I got a Snoopy bedspread. I got every Bruce Lee poster I wanted. She got me excited about it. I don't know how the universe pulled the rabbit out of the hat that is my mom."

Minerva's theory that all change is perceived as loss explains the difficulty of adjusting to a new home. She highly recommends the child be given a say regarding their new room. The input will aid them in dealing with their loss.

"Even with something new, you're saying goodbye to something old. There is an attachment to what she had—it was her safe place. She had her space there, and there was something predictable about that. You've got some control over what this space is going to be. You've got a voice," Minerva says.

Badmouthing the Other Parent

Lisa experienced a true semblance of normalcy for the first time in her life after successfully adjusting to her new home. But once again, Lisa's father—who since his remarriage assumed a more active role in her life—infused doubt in his daughter's mind with his negative comments aimed squarely at Katie.

"I'd go see my dad for the weekend, and I'd be a total asshole to everyone. Mom hated Sundays when I'd come home. I'd be messed up for a whole week," Lisa recalls.

Having seen this kind of behavior in her practice, Minerva cautions that parents shouldn't make it a matter of loyalty for the other person to have a relationship with the kids and to not take it as a betrayal that they still need the other parent—because they do.

"It distorts their ability to have a regular relationship and a bond. If they're getting attention from the parent who had been previously absent, that's going to be really hard to not just want more of, because of course, they want the time and attention. But they're being played," Minerva says.

In Lisa's case, that's exactly what happened on the day she arrived home from school and found a new Schwinn bicycle sitting in the middle of her grandparents' living room. Sporting a big smile, Stan wheeled it across the room and then ceremoniously presented it to his daughter.

In actuality, Katie had bought the bike. Not until Lisa was an adult did her mother explain to her that Stan's only part was delivering the new bike to his parents' house.

"My mom never ever once said one bad thing about my father. She never got defensive and said, 'Oh yeah, your dad did this, or your dad did that.' I don't know how she had the restraint," Lisa says.

Kimberly Shannon, a twenty-nine-year veteran in the world of family counseling, advises divorced parents to restrain from venting their negative feelings about one another in front of their child. "Tuck aside your emotions. Let the child come to terms with their feelings for each parent on their own," Shannon says.

As an adult, Lisa cautions parents to keep their negative feelings to themselves. "It's very, very, important to not cast judgment in front of your child," she says.

Step-relationships

Lisa's visits with her father now included Pam, who eagerly joined in the Katie bashing and also imposed her religious beliefs on Lisa. This resulted in the two constantly butting heads, as it did the day Pam insisted Lisa accompany them to church.

"If you want to be a part of this family, then you *will* attend Sunday services with your father and I," Pam said through clenched teeth.

Lisa moved toward Pam; their faces were nearly touching.

"I am not going anywhere with you, *especially* church," Lisa said, forcing the words from her mouth, one deliberate syllable at a time. "You're not my parent, and nothing you say can change that. I'm only here to see my father."

After that particular fight, Stan must have interceded on Lisa's behalf—although he never admitted that to Lisa—but on her next weekend visit, instead of Pam ranting about her attending Sunday service, Lisa was instead assigned chores to do around the house, putting an end to her battle with Pam. Lisa could not have been happier.

In addition to adjusting to the myriad of personalities that were now a part of her life and her family—a stepfather, stepmother, and stepbrother—Lisa was navigating her way through two vastly different home environments. So much was out of her control that Lisa made changes to the only thing she did have control over—herself.

"I decided to divert my pain into being the class clown. So, I was always the one with the smart-ass remark and always joking around. Just being a real tough girl and hanging out with the boys. I was just a hell raiser," Lisa says.

Lisa's stepbrother was another adjustment to the new family dynamic. Brian regularly spent weekends with his father, which meant Lisa, who by this time had been an only child for ten years, was now dealing with a sibling relationship. And the sibling was someone she barely knew.

"It was interesting, all of a sudden having a brother. It was okay. He was very quiet, though. We would all go to the movies, and he'd go sit by himself. It was really hard to assimilate him," Lisa says with compassion in her voice.

It's safe to assume Brian was dealing with many of the same changes as Lisa—his father's remarriage, the addition of a stepmother, and a new stepsister. Each of them was battling a myriad of internal struggles, so when the opportunity to act out presented itself, each child took advantage of it.

After a weekend stay at her father's, Lisa eagerly leaped up the front porch stairs just as Brian and Bill were leaving the house. Brian stopped for a moment, flashed a grin at his stepsister, and then hopped in his father's car. Lisa stared after them, her face wrinkled in confusion. Normally Brian's mood was either distant or dismissive.

As the car pulled away, Lisa went barreling through the house eager to listen to her new album, stopping just long enough to give her mother an obligatory, "Hi," before heading to her room. She pushed open the door, and her mouth dropped as she surveyed the surroundings. The room looked like it had been hit by the Tasmanian devil. All her toys, cars, puzzles, and books lay scattered and broken on the floor.

Lisa tried side-stepping a pile of discarded toys, doing her best to avoid breaking anything else. But as she tiptoed from one spot to the other, she heard a loud crunch coming from under her right sneaker. She nearly broke into tears when she lifted it and then removed what was left of a shattered glass figurine.

Lisa sprang into action and ran into the Jack and Jill bathroom she and Brian shared. She lifted her stepbrother's Batman toothbrush from its holder and held it in her right hand. She bent down next to the base of the toilet, lowered her right hand into the bowl, and began cleaning the entire surface of the toilet. She spit on the brush and continued diligently cleaning every spot. When she finished, the bowl was spotless.

"And I just put it back and thought, *you little bastard,*" she says, showcasing a wide grin as she recalls that day over four decades ago.

The experts agree integrating two families into one cohesive unit is far from easy, and there is no set time frame for children when it comes to adjusting to the new version of "family." Navigating relationships with the new family members is difficult, and the day-to-day routines shared by each of them may vary as well. The only answer to dealing with these transitions is time. The relationships need to develop at their own pace, and unfortunately, there is no rushing it.

During this adjustment period, Lisa took her frustrations out on her mother and began acting out and saying hurtful remarks to her. Katie's reaction to her daughter's behavior was the same as any parent's—her feelings were hurt. Instead of lashing out at Lisa, she presented her with options: continue living with her and Bill or go live with her father. This unexpected opportunity to choose who and where to live offered Lisa a sense of control in what for her was an ever-changing family dynamic.

"I always had the opportunity to go try it out, and if I didn't like it, I could always come home," Lisa says.

A Time to Let Go

Lisa never chose to exercise the option to live with her father, as his behavior never improved. After a particularly hurtful phone call when Stan, in a drunken state, hurled obscenities at his fifteen-year-old daughter, Lisa severed all ties with him.

Even though Stan passed away over a decade ago, Lisa has never regretted her decision. For Lisa, all that remains are the memories of his mistreatment. Admittedly, she still carries the weight of those incidents, but she no longer carries the negative self-worth he inflicted.

"That was a reflection of him. You get older, and you start to realize stuff like that," she says. "You have to not take on other people's crap, and take it easy on yourself."

Today, Lisa and Katie's relationship is stronger than ever, as are her relationships with Brian and Bill. Lisa, who is gay, is currently single. She realizes that what took place in her youth has had a great impact on the choices she's made regarding past relationships.

"I ended up picking people who were just like my father. I always pick the people who aren't going to accept me. And then I get what I wanted—abandonment or a shitty relationship," Lisa says. "I pick people that there's no way I can be enough for them, like my father. The thing that sucks, even when you're an adult, even at middle age, all that crap lives with me. That's why I'm fifty-six and single. I'm trying to change my thinking and change my life."

She's hopeful that she will soon find a partner to share her life with, one who accepts and supports her. For now, Lisa's content knowing that Katie is a constant in her life, her touchstone. "I could not be who I am today. I don't even know if I'd be surviving today if it weren't for her. And that's a true deal."

My Thoughts

During the time of my divorce, my son was ten years old, and the guilt that came from the realization that I'd stripped him of the only semblance of family he'd ever known weighed heavy on my heart—a burden I carried with me day in and day out.

Over thirty years later, the memory of his big, blue eyes looking up at me, asking, "I don't understand. What's happening, Mom?" still haunts me. Many times I had no answers for him. I often recall his painful journey, especially during the first year after the divorce, as he tried to unravel just what had happened to us all.

During this time, I was struggling as well, trying to come to terms with my failure. With divorce comes blame, and throughout my childhood and marriage, I was the one who accepted the blame for all failures. The divorce was no different. So I bore the entire weight of our family's collapse, accepting the guilt of that failure as penance for finally standing up for my son and myself. Even with the realization that my choice rescued us from an emotionally and physically abusive man, I still felt lost, frightened, and completely uncertain of what was to come, or how I would handle it.

It wasn't until I decided to seek help for my son through counseling that I found help for myself. Through my weekly sessions, I discovered the real me, the me who had been buried under mounds of guilt. Realizing I not only had the right to choose, but the right to live my life my way was a true revelation, but I was still paralyzed by fear.

Uncertain of what lay ahead, just like Katie, I offered my son false reassurance. I kept my fears hidden because, as parents, we want nothing more than to shield our children from all hurt. So instead of sharing the truth, like Katie, I kept it from him. But by disguising our feelings, we cover up our true selves, and really, isn't that all we have to offer? Being honest with our children is important, but being honest with ourselves must come first. This was a lesson learned in hindsight, and a painful one for both my son and I. Honesty with our children, in turn, encourages their honesty with us, and that realization proved to be life-changing for us both. ❤

CHAPTER TWO

MICKEY

Mickey was six years old when his father moved out of the family home. Soon after, his mother became obsessed with seeking vengeance against her ex-husband, with little regard to how her actions affected her only child. Fortunately, Mickey's father remained focused on his son's welfare, providing him the love and support he needed.

❤

Everything Changes

Sitting cross-legged on the floor of his room, six-year-old Mickey stared at Leon Russell's "Back to the Island," his father's prized record, which he'd gifted to his son that morning. Mickey carefully removed the record from its sleeve, placed it on the spindle, and gently set the needle on the edge of the 45. The familiar melody filled the room and drowned out his parents' shouting in the garage—an all too familiar scenario in Mickey's household.

When the record ended, with the melody still resounding in his head, Mickey went to check on his parents. From the garage door, he watched his father load suitcases and boxes into his Chevy Impala, then slam the trunk shut, get into his car, and rev the engine.

Just as the Impala sped out of the driveway, Mickey's mother, Alice, shut the garage door. With the clang of the metal door reverberating in his ears, Mickey watched his mother walk past him, offering no explanation as to where his father was going, or when he'd return.

As Mickey sits in a small coffee shop, his somber tone reflects his lingering melancholy associated with the childhood memory. "I remember that day. It was never good after that," Mickey says.

Stuck in the Middle

After Mickey's father's departure, Alice, who worked full-time at a local grocery store, invited her parents to move in to help look after Mickey. The time he spent with his grandparents provided the young boy many happy memories. Yet, over time, those memories became tainted due to the loyalty they had for their daughter.

"My grandparents just kind of looked out for my mom, took her side, and protected her. They bought into whatever she said," Mickey says.

Alice did everything in her power to minimize the role Mickey's father, Ray, played in his son's life, including limiting his visits to a few hours every other weekend. Even then, she found ways to interfere with the little time they had together.

On one of Ray's scheduled visits, as he was heading out the door on his way to pick Mickey up, the phone rang. When Ray answered it, he was surprised to hear his son's voice on the other end.

"Hi Dad. You're never going to guess where I'm calling from," Mickey said with obvious excitement.

"Where?" Ray asked. "I was just on my way to pick you up."

"We're at the airport. Mom says we're going to Disney Land," Mickey said without taking a breath.

Ray spoke softly yet very distinctly into the receiver. "Let me talk to your mother," he said.

Mickey watched his mother's smile widen as his father's angry voice echoed through the phone. Then she reached out, grabbed her son's hand, and hung up the phone. "Time to go," she said, as she began pulling Mickey through the airport.

Initially, the long periods of separation from his father had little effect on the young boy, but that changed as Mickey got older.

"Probably around nine or ten, that's really when I wanted to start living with my dad," Mickey says. "I always enjoyed being with him. My dad was my hero."

Pitting Child Against Parent

As hurtful as Alice's manipulations were for both Mickey and his father, her consistent badmouthing of Ray in front of her son was equally damaging. This type of behavior, which many times happens with divorced parents, is what Linnea Terranova, founder of Wellspring Psychological Services, calls "the splitting process."

"Splitting is making one person feel awkward or uncomfortable without the other person present," Terranova says. "A child needs to make the decision for himself on how they feel about their parent."

According to the experts, when a child is subject to slandering remarks of one parent by the other, the child's ability to maintain a healthy relationship with that parent becomes distorted and impedes them in securing a healthy parent and child relationship.

Mickey found that to be true, as Ray never retaliated against his ex-wife, and his behavior left a lasting impression on his son. Alice, on the other hand, continued her scheming, each attempt affecting not only Ray but Mickey as well. Such was the case with her strict enforcement of Mickey's agreed upon pick-up times.

"I'd be excited to go see [my dad] and wait by the window, and if he would get there early, my mom would make me wait in the house," Mickey says. "I would just look out the window, waiting."

The same scenario played out when Mickey returned home.

"If my dad was even two minutes late in bringing me back, my mom was on the phone with the cops, telling them that her ex-husband had violated the custody agreement," Mickey says, shaking his head. He added that his grandparents' behavior wasn't much better.

"As I got older, my grandparents kind of got involved in the custody stuff," Mickey says. "My dad would drop me off there, and they would grill me when I got home."

The habitual interrogations not only frustrated Mickey but made him feel guilty for enjoying what little time he had with his father, which led to Mickey's outbursts of yelling and fighting with his mother and grandparents. Alice would then use Mickey's bad behavior as ammunition against Ray.

"They would try and blame it on him, that he was brainwashing me," Mickey says.

Mickey's hostile attitude was a complete contradiction to his congenial personality and caused the young boy to question his own identity.

"I was respectful to my teachers. I was respectful to my parents' friends, to my coaches, and to my dad," Mickey says. "It was just my mom, my grandma and my grandpa. That's who I was acting out against. I would get angry and kind of shut down and take off. I would run away down the street, call my dad, or hide at the store."

According to Collom, acting out is a very common response for children of divorce, as it provides them an outlet for dealing with situations that are totally out of their control.

"Many parents have a lot of bickering and fighting, using the child as a pawn in the continued anger and resentment they have for each other, and that makes it worse for the child," Collom says.

"This type of parental behavior is very dangerous for anyone and most importantly for a child that's trying to understand their world that's been broken," Terranova adds.

Mickey Makes a Choice

Alice's determination to break the bond between father and son continued for the next six years, which provided Mickey a clear insight into her deceitful ways.

"I was about ten or eleven, in fifth grade when all the dots just totally connected," Mickey says.

This realization prompted heated arguments between mother and son, severely damaging their relationship. The disconnect with his mother strengthened Mickey's desire to spend more time with Ray and prompted his decision to spend his summer vacation at his dad's.

"It was kind of a test to see if this was what I wanted to do," Mickey says.

When summer ended, Mickey had to make a choice—stay with his father and start sixth grade at a new school—or return to his mother's. Mickey's ties to his old school ultimately swayed his decision.

"I grew up with all my friends and my sports and my teams," Mickey says in defense of his choice.

Not long after he moved back to his mother's, Mickey realized he'd made a bad choice. During breakfast on the first day of baseball tryouts, Alice informed her son that she'd decided he was no longer allowed to try out for the team.

Mickey dropped his spoon in the half-empty cereal bowl and glared across the table at her. "What do you mean I can't go to baseball tryouts? You know I'll make the team," Mickey pushed his chair away from the table and stood up.

"I forbid you to go. End of story," Alice said, taking a sip of her morning coffee.

Mickey headed to the garage. "I'm going, and you can't stop me," he shouted.

Alice sprinted across the kitchen and grabbed her son by the shoulders as he came through the door.

"You're not going anywhere except to your room," she said.

Mickey ran to his room, tears streaming down his cheeks. Staring at the shelves lined with toys, he spotted the Hot Wheels cars. Mickey gathered them up and flung them at the doorway where his mother stood.

Alice walked over to her son and slapped him across the face. Mickey stared at his mother—she'd never hit him before. As he rubbed his fingers along the sore spot on his cheek, his face flushed and his eyes widened. Turning behind him, he grabbed his baseball bat, raised it, and pointed it at her.

"Hit me now," Mickey said, his smile transforming into a sneer.

Alice ran to the front door, Mickey just a few steps behind her. Once she escaped the house, he threw himself against the door and locked it, then ran back to his room, collapsed on his bed, and cried himself to sleep.

Later, when Mickey woke, two police officers and a counselor stood on one side of his bed and his mother and grandfather on the other. Ignoring them all, he jumped up and ran to the living room, grabbed the phone and called his father. A few hours later, Ray arrived and Mickey met him at the door with his suitcase in hand.

"This was on a Saturday, and Monday we went down to the new school and signed me up," Mickey says. My dad never pressured me to come with him. He said if [moving in with him] was something I ever wanted, to let him know. He was solid."

A New Start

Living with Ray offered Mickey an atmosphere of mutual respect and love, something he never experienced with his mother.

"Once I lived with my dad and started a new school, I made friends right away. I got right into sports," Mickey says.

His new living arrangement also provided him the opportunity to get to know his stepmother, Rachel. And a few years later, he eagerly accepted the role of big brother when his half-sister, Claire, was born.

Although the transition to his new home went smoothly, Alice once again interfered, when only a few days later she called Ray and demanded Mickey return home. Ray's response was clear and concise: "He's here, and he's going to school."

"That's when my dad started fighting in court, and everything just exploded," Mickey said. "It was a fight from that weekend on."

Ray's defiance intensified Alice's vengeance, which she exacted by targeting Ray's character, accusing him of child abuse and neglect. Her accusations resulted in court-mandated family counseling sessions, as well as one-on-one sessions for Mickey, which proved beneficial to the young boy.

"[The therapist's] name was Rodney, and I loved the guy. He kind of made me want to get into that field," Mickey says. "He was great. He really kind of advocated for me. I felt like he had my side. I had a voice."

For the next four years, until Mickey was sixteen, Alice continued her court battles, subjecting Mickey to countless court appearances and slanderous accusations against his father. After one such incident, Mickey had had enough.

"I remember just screaming, SHE'S LYING, SHE'S LYING!" Mickey says.

A child's involvement in court battles should be avoided at all costs, as experts' caution it may prove to be psychologically damaging to the child.

Collom explains, "Keeping a united front helps them with the transition."

"Children need a healthy relationship with both their parents," Minerva adds. "That's not always possible, but it is still what should be ideal and what people should strive for," she says.

Alice's continued attempts to win her son back resulted in Mickey agreeing to visit her on the weekends. But that wasn't enough for Alice, who soon returned to her old ways.

After his mother left for work, Mickey gathered his football helmet and duffel bag and called to his grandparents.

"We need to get going. I don't want to be late for football practice," he said.

Mickey watched his grandparents walk toward him, their faces stern.

"Your mother told us not to let you go," his grandfather said. "She's your mother. You must do as you are told."

Mickey stared at the elderly couple, who avoided his eyes.

"Fine, I'll get there myself," Mickey said as he exited the house, slamming the door behind him.

Ten minutes later he boarded a bus. Not long after, it came to an abrupt stop, and Mickey watched two police officers get on the bus. After a brief conversation with the driver, they made their way down the aisle. They stopped when they reached Mickey.

"Mickey Landers, you need to come with us," one officer said.

Too frightened to ask what was happening, Mickey followed their instructions and got into the back seat of their car. A few minutes later, the car stopped at his house, where his mother stood waiting for him.

He immediately jumped out of the car. "I am not going back to my mother's, ever," Mickey shouted as his eyes teared up.

Alice signaled to her father, a retired police captain, who then instructed the officers. "Do as my daughter says."

"My son's in contempt of the custody agreement," Alice said. "I want you to take him to Juvenile Hall."

Mickey's mouth dropped open as the officers made their way towards him. The shorter one opened the backseat door, then gestured for him to get inside. They drove in silence until they reached a large gray building with a sign that read: Juvenile Center Entrance.

"This is your stop, son," the officer said as he opened the car door.

Mickey followed in silence as the officers escorted him to the front desk, where a female guard gestured for him to turn around. After turning his back, he felt the cold steel of handcuffs being secured to his wrists.

"Let's go," she said, her tone flat but forceful.

Mickey followed her down a long hallway of green metal doors. When they reached door number 128, the guard stopped. Staring inside the stark windowless room meagerly furnished with a cot and a toilet, Mickey began to shake. He couldn't stop. Just as the guard was ushering him inside, a familiar voice called out.

"Mickey, what are you doing here?" the voice asked.

A moment later, Mickey found himself standing face to face with his high school football coach—who also worked as a probation officer. Making a valiant effort to keep his voice steady, Mickey explained to Coach Stevens what happened. After which, Stevens signaled to the guard who nodded and then released Mickey from his handcuffs. Mickey then followed Stevens to his office, where he placed a call to Ray. Although Ray was not home, Rachel assured him she would be there as soon as she could.

"You should be home by supper time, Mickey," Stevens said as he clapped the boy on his shoulder.

Less than an hour later, Rachel arrived. "I'm so, so, sorry you had to go through this, Mickey," Rachel said. "Let's get you home."

Mickey shakes his head, then takes a long sip of his coffee.

"From that point on, I didn't see my mom," he says. "She would call, and I was supposed to see her, but I just refused."

Enough is Enough

Although Alice made numerous attempts to connect with her son, including sending a police car to Ray's house, Mickey remained consistent—he no longer wanted anything to do with her. For the next three years, he held fast to his decision, but his mother never gave up, and finally, Mickey conceded and met up with her.

"I had my driver's permit, and I was driving with her, and we got into it, and I called my cousins to come pick me up," Mickey says.

Once again, Alice called the police on her son and instructed them to take him to a local children's shelter. When the shelter realized Mickey was brought to them under false pretenses, Ray was notified, and Mickey returned home.

At this point, there was no turning back. Mickey wanted

nothing more to do with his mother. Unfortunately, this decision marked the end of his relationship with his grandparents, as they continued to arrange for Alice to be present each time Mickey visited them, even though he'd expressed to them both that he no longer wanted anything to do with her.

"I think what bothers me the most is losing that relationship with my grandparents. They loved me. They did everything for me. It was tough," Mickey says.

After graduating from high school, Mickey enrolled in college and pursued a career in social work. While still in school, he secured a position at a children's center as a residential counselor, providing support for troubled kids and teens, something Mickey could relate to.

"I always knew I was going to do something with kids," Mickey says.

Throughout his ten years at the center, Mickey worked his way from a residential counselor up to director of marketing and communications and continues to devote his career to the non-profit sector. Even though Ray moved out of state, Mickey's relationship with his father remains intact. When it comes to his mother, considering the deterioration of her health throughout the years, Mickey realizes she may have always had some type of mental condition. Still, her imprint on his life is one that will never be erased

"She is who she is, and she affects my life zero," Mickey says. "She doesn't cross my mind."

*If a spouse or loved one is suffering from mental health issues, Mental Health America advises you to seek help. "Get names of mental health professionals from your doctor, friends, clergy, or local Mental Health America affiliates."

My Thoughts

As hard as we try to overcome the prejudices we feel towards our exes, too many times we fail, and it's our children who pay the price for our unbridled restraint. I'd accumulated over twelve years of resentment and anger toward my ex-husband by the time we divorced. Although I made every effort to keep from voicing my negative remarks about him to my son, I'm certain my true feelings showed through.

So how do you protect your child from your negative feelings for your ex? There is no easy solution, but when dealing with the fragility of your child's feelings, you have to find a way. I found mine through counseling. Having the opportunity to vent my true feelings about his father in therapy was incredibly freeing.

Through my therapist, I found a safe place where I didn't have to think before I spoke; I could just let go of every hurtful thought and every angry feeling—of which there were many—and surprisingly, I found that release was enough. I didn't need confirmation. I didn't need to seek vengeance against him, as Alice did. What I needed most—was to be heard.

Reaching that safe place took time, and my journey was slow, but I did get there. When I finally arrived, I allowed myself the luxury of focusing on myself, and not only did that help me, it allowed me to help my son. The freedom of unburdening the negativity that had ruled our lives for so long allowed me to offer my son a healthier version of our family—one we both deserved. ♥

CHAPTER THREE

TONY

One person's actions can make a difference. In Tony's case, his mother's actions left him and his older sister children of divorce. The family was torn apart, and with no explanation for her departure, the siblings and their father were left to bear the burden of blame.

Tony was a bit guarded in disclosing the events that took place in his family over a decade ago. The details he did share, though brief, reveal a man still searching for answers while doing his best to move forward with his life.

❤

The Phone Call

After a long day of construction, dressed in his usual work attire, jeans and a chambray shirt rolled up at the sleeves, Tony headed home to unwind. He opened the door to his '95 red two-door Mustang, which released a wave of sweltering heat, then slid behind the wheel and lowered the driver side window. Tilting his head back, Tony welcomed the summer breeze as it floated through the car and tickled his chin. After starting the engine, he tuned the radio to his favorite rock station, WKNG, and headed out of the parking lot.

The job site was only eight miles from his home, so he traveled the side streets, passing the local market where he worked part-time when he was a freshman in college. Continuing down Louis Avenue, Tony passed Greenfield High, where he'd graduated over a decade ago. Approaching Sixth Street, he turned right, and minutes later arrived at the familiar three-story apartment building. The complex—which he'd moved to on his twenty-fifth birthday—offered affordable rates and a friendly neighborhood.

After parking in the underground garage, Tony pocketed the keys and took the elevator to the third floor. Stepping into the hallway, he was immediately enveloped by the scent of curry, which hung heavy in the air. The familiar aroma—one that brought a smile to his lips—signaled to him that his neighbor, Mrs. Kaball, was making her famous chicken Kiev, one she always shared with Tony. Nearing his apartment, he heard the familiar ring of his phone and stepped up his pace, but as he slid his key into the lock, the ringing ceased.

Once inside, it rang again. Lifting the receiver to his ear, he heard his sister's shaky and hoarse voice.

"Tony, Mom took off. Took all her stuff. Left notes and took Grandpa's car," Sherry explained in a rush.

Tony stood in silence, the phone clutched in his hand.

"Did you hear me? Mom's gone," his sister repeated.

Shaking his head, Tony realized he needed to speak.

"I heard you. How's Dad?"

As Tony hung up the phone, he felt as though he'd just been punched in the gut. He reached out, grabbed a chair, and slowly sat down. He couldn't imagine how his father felt.

Confronting Loss

Slipping his lean frame into the booth, his tanned and sinewy arm flexes as he picks up his cup and takes a sip of his latte, making it hard to detect Tony's unease, although it's there—the twitch of his dark eyes—the repeated clearing of his throat as he recalls past events. His one-word answer to the question: "What did you need most from your mother during this time?" makes that clear.

"Answers," he says in a steely tone.

Tony readily admits his mother's departure was a shock, not only to him but his entire family. He also admits she was "acting weird leading up to it."

"She left like a thief in the night," Tony says. "Wanted nothing more to do with this life or family. Dad got a note. Sister got a note. *I* got nothing."

Tony closes his eyes and pauses briefly, recalling the memory of his mother's failure to leave her only son a goodbye note. The silent moments that follow indicate those long-ago hurts are wounds that still sting.

"Don't know if she did things out of spite or not, but the fact that she took my grandpa's Lincoln was like someone twisting the knife they just stabbed you with."

Tony fails to recall—or chooses not to remember—the events that transpired after he heard the news from his sister. He does vividly recall meeting up with his father at church a few days after his mother's departure. Bent over the soundboard, Tony made a final check of the equipment, ensuring it was set up for the following week's service. Hearing the sound of footsteps, heavy and slow, he turned and found his father, Bert, standing behind him, his face solemn and pale.

"You did a really good job mixing everything, son," Bert said, making a valid effort to keep his voice level.

"Dad, are you OK?" Tony asked.

"No," his father said, with a catch in his throat.

Bert's eyes welled as the two men stared at one another. Tony, having witnessed his father reduced to such an emotional state only once before—the day his grandfather, Bert's father died—had no words, so he gestured to the stairs, and the two men walked in silence to the church lobby. Before heading out the front door, Dorothy Poster, one of his mother's friends, waved and then hurried over to join them.

"Bert, where's the missus?" Dorothy said, turning her gray-haired head side to side.

"She's gone, Dorothy. She left me," Bert said before he turned away.

Without a word, Bert took the lead, and Tony followed as they exited the church. They continued in silence across the parking lot, and when they reached Bert's car, Tony threw his arms around his father's neck and listened in silence to his muffled sobs. A few minutes later, Bert slowly pulled away, and Tony pointed to his car on the opposite end of the lot.

Bert nodded, wiped his eyes, and then got in his car. Minutes later, Tony sat behind the Mustang's steering wheel, watching his father begin his long drive home alone.

"That day broke my heart," Tony says, shaking his head and taking a long sip of his drink. "I pride myself in the fact that I can fix a lot of things, but I couldn't do anything in that situation. He's normally a very rock-solid person. He was absolutely floored, had no idea this was coming. I have always looked up to him. It was hard to see him broken. Felt helpless. Still hurts to think about. Poor guy was left to answer all the hard questions."

Residual Feelings

The memories of that pivotal day cause a change in Tony's voice; a resounding tone of bitterness is evident as he talks about his mother's actions.

"She showed a complete lack of respect for the entire family," Tony says. "It was very one-sided and selfish, trying to put the blame on everyone and not owning any of the responsibilities."

Now a husband and father of two, Tony finds it impossible to comprehend his mother's motivation to leave her family, making her decision even more painful for him.

"Having kids now, I couldn't imagine willfully leaving them, no matter their age," he says.

Reticent to provide details of how he and his family moved past his mother's departure, Tony is eager to share his feelings for his father.

"I love my father and thank him for being so strong in such a terrible situation," Tony says. "I thank him for not just giving up and walking away when things got tough. He's a great role model, and he inspires me to be the man I try to be every day."

Tony is reluctant to share the details, but prior to her abandonment, his mother proved a source of friction between him and his father. With her departure came the ability to repair their relationship and create an unbreakable bond between father and son. Tony credits Bert as one of the strongest men he knows, although he's painfully aware that not only was his father emotionally wounded by his mother's actions, he was physically affected as well.

"I still think his heart surgeries were a result of the divorce," Tony says. "I think a heart can be broken."

With little communication from his mother other than the occasional email, Tony still wrestles with the question: Why did she leave?

"She has three grandkids she'll probably never see again," Tony says. "Two of which she's never met. Obviously, things were going on, (although he's unclear as to what they were), and she wasn't all there, but just like I tell my five-year-old, I can't help if I don't know what's wrong."

Tony's lingering regret that his mother never came to him for help before she left is evident in the softness of his voice. It's a question that may never be answered. Experts agree a commonality experienced by children of divorce, no matter the age, is the feeling of loss.

"We feel that abandonment, and we feel helpless. We're right back to that hurt child," licensed marriage and family therapist, Eleanor Scott, says, adding that many times the problem the adult child [of divorce] doesn't understand is that they have the power to heal from their wounds.

"We get to rescript, we get to figure out how we want to live our life," Scott says.

Tony, unlike the majority of children of divorce, carries no guilt regarding his parents' divorce, placing it entirely on his mother.

"There was nothing that anyone other than my mom could have done to change the situation," he says. "The choice was already made for all of us."

Even without the burden of blame, Tony cautions children of divorce, no matter their age, to reach out for help. That's what Tony did.

"Even though it's not your fault, the situation has a way of breaking you," Tony says. "Surround yourself with people that build you up. You'll need that more than anything. Friends, siblings, and loved ones will be your rock."

Scott advises focusing on building internal resources. "As adults, we have the opportunity to heal from our wounds by doing our own work, and that can be challenging; it's a lot of work, a lot of energy and time," she says.

According to Scott, past hurts remain a part of us, and as adults, we try to mend those wounds through relationships. "We want somebody else to heal that wound, and the only one who can is the person themselves. It's really our healing, our work that has to happen," Scott says.

It's Never Easy

Tony believes his age at the time of his parents' divorce made it easier on him, but he's quick to add that no matter the age, "[divorce] is devastating across the board."

"Kids, unfortunately, don't really understand the reason why, which always seems to make them feel like they are partly responsible when in fact, it's solely on the parents," Tony says. "Young adults tend to understand this a bit more, in my opinion. Divorce is very cutting. The scars I got when I was young have been with me the longest, and I remember those stories the most. The older you are when this situation pokes its ugly head, the easier I think you have it in the long run. But it still sucks, regardless."

Support

Even though Tony and his sister, Sherry, were never close, having someone to go through the family's breakup did make a difference. "She was still there for me," Tony says.

Experts agree that siblings many times deal with a parents' divorce differently. That's been the case with Sherry.

"She tucked it away, and things that should be small are getting stacked on top of it," Tony says. "Everything that should be small and brushed off is getting amplified in a way that isn't healthy. It is causing ripples in her marriage. Instead of getting help or talking about it, she just holds onto it."

Luckily for Tony, he had Ann, his girlfriend at the time and now his wife, as an additional source of support.

"She was awesome through the whole thing," Tony says. "Her family was my extended family, and I am forever grateful."

Now nearing forty, Tony has had over a decade to heal, and that healing has manifested itself in a sincere hope of happiness for both his parents. Although he's quick to add, he's certain they will never find it together.

"I think hell has a better chance of freezing over before that happens," Tony says, giving me a quick grin and then exiting the booth.

My Thoughts

Divorce affects every child, no matter the age, just as it did for Tony. By surrounding himself with loved ones, Tony provided himself the support he needed, which was a crucial part of his healing. Tony has successfully moved forward in his life, marrying his perfect partner and building a family together. He can't change his parents' divorce, and although he still carries that loss, he's admittedly very content with his life.

My son is near Tony's age and has lived over three decades with the imprint of his parents' divorce. He has little to no communication with his father, and like Tony, he has reached a point where he wants to move on from the hurt and pain of the past to heal. To do that, he seeks closure from his father in any form he can find it. So far, his attempts have been unsuccessful, but I know my son, and he's not ready to quit trying.

Standing on the sidelines watching him wrestle with unresolved feelings is painful, but that pain is offset by my pride in his willingness to move forward with his life regardless of past wounds. Being the product of a divorced family will always be an actuality of my son's life, but that fact does not define his life or him. Acceptance of the past allows for a clear focus on the future and the choices it brings. For my son, for Tony, and for all children of divorce, where there's a choice, there is always hope. ❤

CHAPTER FOUR

ELLEN

Ellen was eight years old when her parents divorced, and her father moved out of the family home. Fear resulting from this change in the family dynamic became an ongoing struggle for Ellen, especially during pivotal times in her life. When those fears resurfaced, they were accompanied by an undercurrent of anger that Ellen refused to acknowledge until it was too late.

The Moment of Reality

Sitting on the edge of her bed in baggy sweatpants and a wrinkled T-shirt, Ellen gently rocked back and forth while twisting the ends of her matted blond hair. Her eyes were fixated across the room at a poster of a kitten clinging to a rope, the words, Hang In there Baby, below it. The college freshman was oblivious to the clamor of students gathered at the entrance to her dorm room.

After countless attempts to break Ellen's trance, her roommate Stacey, went for help. Marjorie Brennan, the freshman guidance counselor, knocked lightly on Ellen's door before entering the room.

"Ellen, how are you doing?" Marjorie asked. "You've missed your first two classes."

Ellen's gaze remained on the poster as a faint smile spread across her lips.

"He's not going to make it," Ellen said, releasing her hair from her fingers and pointing to the wall.

"Ellen, I need you to tell me how you're feeling," Marjorie said, her voice rising despite her attempt to remain calm.

Ellen's shoulders began to shake as she turned her tear-stained face to the woman who stood at the end of her bed.

"I can't let them do this to me anymore," she said, releasing a low guttural moan like that of a wounded animal.

"Will you help me?"

Sitting in her kitchen with the late afternoon sunlight starting to fade, Ellen, now in her late thirties, reflects on the moment she realized she could no longer allow her family's needs to outweigh her own.

"I had to experience so many adult things: their dating game, separate holidays and birthdays, stepparents, stepsiblings, more divorce, constantly moving, being passed back and forth between my mom and dad," Ellen says as she adjusts her legs and wipes her eyes.

Ellen's anger began with her parents' separation, and although she doesn't remember an official announcement, she does recall how she felt during those early days.

"I remember that period of time when it was occurring, and the situations we were put in and my dad moving out and staying at friends," Ellen says. "It was horrible, and I think it really affected us. It's almost like your whole world is just turned upside down, and you're split three ways or four ways; I don't even know how many ways."

Countless times being dragged into her parents' lives, expected to help sort out their problems, which included extramarital affairs, no matter what was happening in her life, fueled Ellen's anger.

"I felt like I had to be the adult. I was robbed of my childhood. I had to grow up really fast," Ellen says. It's almost like my whole life I've been catering to each one of them and what they want and what they prefer."

But it wasn't until years later—that day in her dorm room—that Ellen acknowledged her anger.

"I just pushed down all of my feelings and didn't really understand the emotions I was feeling. I had so much anger toward my dad, and I had so much anger toward my mom."

The realization of her family's selfishness resulted in a serious mental breakdown for Ellen. After months of medical treatment and weekly therapy sessions, she learned the importance of addressing her anger.

Collom explains that the ongoing effects of divorce follow children throughout their adulthood.

"Especially if the feelings have been repressed, locked, and left in the closet," Collom says. "Those unconscious places that we haven't dealt with impact us, and divorce is one of those."

Parental Expectations

An unexpected result of her parents' divorce was the disclosure of a long-hidden secret—her older brother Tom was actually Ellen and her sister Tina's half-brother.

"That was a hard concept to grasp," Ellen says. "My mother was only in high school when she got pregnant with my brother, and with her mother's consent, she married his dad when she was seventeen."

Once the secret was revealed, Ellen's father, Richard, no longer felt obligated to cover up his true feelings for Tom.

"My dad didn't want to have anything to do with him," Ellen says, with a slight quiver in her voice. "That was really hard for me to watch because it really hurt my brother and made me look at my dad in a different light."

Although Richard's behavior exposed his selfish nature, Ellen still loved her father, even when his selfishness interfered with her personal life. Such was the case the day her friend called.

"Dad, guess what?" Ellen said, smiling as she hung up the phone. "Sandy wants me to come over to her house. Can I go?"

Richard turned his back on his daughter and walked out of the room. Ellen followed him, a sinking feeling of queasiness overtaking her.

"It will only be for a little while," Ellen said in a whisper.

They walked to the living room in silence. Richard took a seat in his brown leather recliner and then leaned back and released an audible sigh.

"You'd rather spend time with your friends than with me," he said. "I guess you might as well go."

He grabbed the remote off the table, and Ellen watched in silence as the greenish glow of the screen reflected on her father's face. Shoulders slumped, she walked over to his chair, knelt down, and then leaned her head against his arm.

"It's OK, Dad, I don't have to go. I'd rather stay with you," Ellen said, her throat tightening.

Richard patted his daughter's face and smiled. "That's a good girl," he said.

A parent's tendency to lose sight of their primary concern—their child's needs—is a common byproduct of divorce. Ellen experienced this behavior not only with her father but with her mother as well. After the break-up, Nora made weekly trips to the gym in an attempt to create a new look for herself. This physical transformation resulted in a constant parade of boyfriends visiting the house nearly every night of the week, leaving the brunt of the family's responsibilities solely on Ellen's shoulders.

"I need you to fix dinner for your sister," Nora said as she brushed past her daughter on her way to the front door. "You're going out again?" Ellen asked as she stared at her mother's latest outfit, a dark blue tube top, black mini-skirt, and three-inch stiletto heels.

"I'm just meeting Jimmy for a quick drink. I'll be back in time to tuck you girls into bed," Nora said as she blew her daughter a kiss and then opened the door. Ellen rushed to the door and blocked it with her body, all ninety pounds of it.

"You said that last night *and* the night before," Ellen said. "You're never home anymore."

Nora's unrelenting stare remained fixed on her daughter as she moved her out of the way.

"What's wrong with doing what I want to do for a change?" Nora said as she exited the house, slamming the door behind her.

During this time of upheaval, the most confusing part for Ellen was that neither parent seemed to comprehend the devastating effect their actions had on her.

"It's almost like my parents weren't educated, or no one told them what they're doing was wrong, or that they just didn't know,"

Ellen says. "It's weird that they come from divorced parents too. I just don't understand why they didn't learn anything from their parents and how they felt."

Counseling is Not for Everyone

Soon after the divorce, Tina's behavior began to spiral out of control. Nora sought family counseling. Unfortunately, the sessions provided little benefit for Ellen, who recalls how both she and Tom spent the entire hour "laughing and messing around."

According to Collom, Ellen's reaction was not unusual.

"Not all children need it or want it," Collom explains. "Sometimes they don't even know how they feel."

Instead of one-on-one sessions, Collom recommends children attend group sessions, and cautions parents to never force a child into therapy. Although therapy wasn't a beneficial resource for Ellen, that didn't mean she wasn't in need of support. The two people she counted on most—her parents—were not emotionally available for her during this difficult time.

Family Dynamics

Two years after the divorce, Richard remarried. Initially, Ellen was happy for her father, but his expectation that she accept her stepmother unconditionally proved difficult. With the addition of her half-siblings and her father's attention focused solely on his new family, she began to feel as though she had no place in his life.

Scott explains this type of behavior is common with men when they remarry.

"When a man remarries and starts a new family, he's less engaged in his previous family," Scott says. "I think a part of it is that men don't necessarily have the skills to navigate that. How do I make peace with my kids who are really mad at me?"

Feeling that her relationship with her father was at an end, Ellen's fears escalated, and her self-worth diminished.

"We felt like more of a burden to our stepmom and their new family, and my dad never defended us on that notion," Ellen says. "I think my dad felt torn between making this perfect family with his new wife and being a father to us."

Ellen believes her father's attempts to placate her and Tina by buying them extravagant gifts is evidence that he was well aware of how his lack of attention affected them. Yet his behavior never changed.

"Even to this day, the loss of my dad is devastating to me," Ellen says. "I always felt like I wasn't good enough to be his number one priority. As a child, I was confused and sad and starving for his attention and love, and I didn't understand."

According to Minerva, children tend to blame themselves in this type of situation.

"The children are going to feel like there's something wrong with them that the parent isn't there," Minerva says.

In addition to Richard's lack of attention, Nora, who married and divorced twice by the time Ellen was eighteen, had her own expectations.

"So, through my high school years, I had different stepdads and stepsiblings that were in and out of my life," Ellen says. "And it was really hard because you have to grow up super fast, and you almost feel alone all the time because you never have that sense of stability."

Nora's inability to understand her daughter's reluctance to embrace each new iteration of the family fueled Ellen's anger all the more.

"There was no way in hell I was going to embrace another family and have it get ripped out from under me *again*," Ellen says. "I think the older I was getting, I was mad. I was furious."

Putting the Child in the Middle

In addition to her parents' unrealistic expectations, Ellen felt she was being used as a pawn in their ongoing battles, even on the day of her high school graduation.

After changing out of her cap and gown, Ellen crossed the hall to join her parents, feeling confident that today—her graduation day—their attention would be focused solely on her for a change.

"What did you think of the ceremony?" Ellen said with a smile.

Nora quickly turned away from Richard and focused her attention on her daughter.

"It was lovely, dear, but now it's time to head home for your party," Nora said, grabbing Ellen's arm.

"Wait just a minute," Richard interjected. "My little girl is coming with me. Everyone's already at the house."

Ellen shook free of her mother's hold and stared at her father in disbelief.

"Both of you are throwing me a party—on the same day?" Ellen said, rolling her eyes. "How can I be at two places at once?"

Nora was quick to provide her daughter with an answer. "You can't. So you'll be coming home with me," she said as she reached for Ellen.

Richard took a step forward and blocked Nora's grasp and then grabbed his daughter's hand. "I've invited all your friends, so you don't want to miss *my* party," Richard said.

Nora sidestepped Richard and stood directly in front of her daughter.

"All the family is waiting for you at the house. I know you don't want to let them down," Nora countered, her smile morphing into a sad pout.

Ellen let go of her father's hand and moved out of her mother's reach. "I don't believe you two. Even on my graduation day, it's still all about you," Ellen said. "This is what we're going to do. First, I'll go to Mom's and spend a few hours there. Then, I'll head over to your house, Dad," Ellen said as she grabbed her mother's hand and led her out of the building.

Escape from Responsibility

The end of high school meant escape for Ellen as she'd chosen a college that required her to live away from home. For the first time in her life, she was free of her family and able to focus on herself. But before the end of her freshman year, the emotional turmoil her family had inflicted on her over the years surfaced. The mental breakdown in her dorm room that year led Ellen to seek professional help. With weekly counseling sessions, she started to understand the importance of acknowledging her feelings.

By the time Ellen graduated from college, she was eager to move forward. She moved to the East Coast in pursuit of a career in event planning, but unfortunately, her plans didn't work out as she'd hoped, and the following year she returned home. Out of necessity, she temporarily moved in with her father and stepmother. Her father's behavior and lack of attention, which remained focused on his wife and younger children, triggered a return of Ellen's feelings of rejection and loss.

This time Ellen recognized what was happening to her and took action. She again sought professional counseling, and through it received confirmation that she was suffering from an anxiety disorder. Resuming therapy helped Ellen control her anxiety issues, which brought her a renewed sense of confidence. For the first time in her life, she considered the possibility of a long-term relationship and immediately reached out to Phil, her college roommate's brother.

From the moment they met in college, there was an immediate attraction, but Phil was in a relationship at the time, so neither acted on their feelings. After connecting with Phil on social media, they soon began dating. Six months later, they moved in together, and not long after that there was talk of marriage. What should have been one of the happiest days of her life—the day Phil proposed—Ellen's fears and insecurities resurfaced.

"I literally remember sitting there making lists to make sure he was the right one," Ellen says. "I looked at what my life would look like."

In addition to her doubts, Ellen's potential in-laws were unsupportive, citing Ellen's family history as a cause for their concern.

"And so it almost makes me resent my family even more. Because my parents are divorced, I am not deserving," Ellen says.

The sting of her future in-laws' rejection caused Ellen to dig her heels in to prove to them their fears were unwarranted.

"I am not sure I ever won them over, more like they realized that I wasn't going anywhere," Ellen says, with a wave of her hand. "At that point, they opened up and got to know me, and I found my place in the family."

Ellen's efforts to prove herself worthy solidified her certainty that marrying Phil was something she sincerely wanted. As happy as she was on her wedding day, the transition to married life was a difficult one for Ellen.

"When I married my husband, I was really excited, but it was a process for me," Ellen says.

She readily admits the crux of the problems stemmed from her fears and doubts. Her parents' divorce, followed by her mother's subsequent marriages and divorces, made the idea of a happily ever after a challenging concept for Ellen to accept, even though it was one she longed for.

Taking a good look at her marriage, Ellen realized there was one major difference between her parents' marriage and hers. She and Phil were committed to maintaining and improving their relationship, something she didn't see modeled by her parents. That realization brought Ellen a true sense of security.

"We work very hard at acknowledging each of our raw spots. It is work for sure, but I wouldn't want to do it with anyone else," Ellen says.

Standing up for Herself

Ellen's adjustment to her new life was additionally hampered by her parents' disapproval of her in-laws. Thanks to years of therapy, Ellen had reached a point where she was aware of the negative repercussions of hiding her true feelings. This left her no choice but to stand up for herself and her marriage, which is what she did the day she invited her parents to her house.

Once they arrived, Ellen directed them to the kitchen, where they each took a seat. Nora chose a chair at the small kitchen table while Richard perched—as though he was ready to flee at a moment's notice—on a stool at the breakfast bar. Straightening her shoulders, Ellen faced them both and wasted no time.

"I'm done," Ellen said, her heart racing. "I'm tired of playing your games. My relationship with my in-laws isn't any of your business," she said. "I have my own life to focus on, my own family, and I have every intention to make that my top priority. I won't let either of you destroy that. I will no longer be your rock."

Richard remained silent, while Nora stared at her daughter, who was making an unsuccessful attempt to steady her shaking hands.

"You've never spoken this way before. You're so upset," Nora said, her voice calm but sincere. "Have we really been that bad?"

Ellen didn't even try to stifle a laugh. Richard immediately stood up and then marched past his daughter.

"You have no right to speak to me this way. I am your father, and I deserve your respect," he said, pushing past her and then out of the room.

A few moments later, the front door slammed shut.

The confrontation proved successful for Ellen, as it helped ease her anger towards her parents, and in its place, she found compassion for them both.

"I almost feel sad for them because they're just miserable," Ellen says. "They're just not happy people."

Ellen's declaration did not change her relationship with her father, who continued to hand off the responsibility of maintaining their relationship squarely on Ellen's shoulders.

"I feel like he puts his guilt and responsibilities on me," Ellen says.

Nora was much more receptive to her daughter's honesty.

"So now I accept my relationship with my mom and don't take on my siblings' issues and just enjoy helping my mom cope by listening and being there for her," Ellen says.

Grieving and Loss

Ellen and Phil are entering their tenth year of marriage and have two sons, ages seven and five. Just as in the past, when confronted with significant changes, each of Ellen's pregnancies brought a resurgence of insecurity in addition to serious bouts of postpartum depression.

"In the back of my mind, I'm always worried about abandonment, like is this going to work out? So, I think that feeling carries with you forever," Ellen says.

According to Shannon, children ages seven and up develop concrete operations in their thinking and begin to understand the concept that death is permanent. So when a marriage dies, a child mourns.

"Kids, as with any individual, when they have a trauma in their life will go through the phases of death and dying. It's the loss of the family unit," Shannon says.

For Ellen, that loss has permeated all aspects of her life.

"My biggest fear in life, now that I have two little boys, is what if we get divorced or if our marriage is not a good role model for them," Ellen says. "I would never want my kids to go through what I went through. When my parents divorced I believe a lot died. I believe my childhood innocence was dead. Any sort of stability was dead. My family and sense of togetherness was dead. My childhood home was dead and none of this was ever rebuilt in my childhood. I think the worst part is most of the positive memories I have are dead, and I seem to only remember or revisit the bad parts."

Now that Ellen is a mother and wife, she's added to her list of losses.

"Respect for my parents is dead. Looking at them as positive role models is dead. Looking to them for advice on parenting and marriage is dead. Family traditions to carry on with my children are dead," Ellen says.

Will Ellen ever reach a point where she'll be able to move on from her losses? She holds onto the hope that someday she will.

"I try to stay positive and take what I can from my experiences and learn from my parents' mistakes," Ellen says. "But if I am honest with myself, it all still hurts, and I'm still angry, and it does depress me at times. Like the death of a loved one, the feelings won't ever go away, but I just learn to accept it all a little more every day and move forward."

My Thoughts

It's understandable for parents to lose sight of their children's needs while wading through the legal and emotional battles of divorce. As a parent trying to maintain a sense of normalcy in what quickly escalated into a world of chaos and pain, I made every effort to project a persona of strength and confidence in the hope that I was shielding my child from additional trauma. But was that a realistic goal?

I'm not so sure. First, my son witnessed his father move out of the family home only to relocate into a new one—three blocks away. Then, on his father's weekends, he was subjected to a line of questioning regarding my whereabouts, forcing our son in the role of spy. How could he *not* be affected by this?

As for me, I invited a female friend of mine to move in with us as it provided an in-house babysitter when I secured a full-time job. Suddenly, someone my son saw on an infrequent basis became a part of our daily household and someone who told him what he could and could not do. My expectations, as was the case with Ellen's parents, was for him to accept all these changes willingly, without question.

In all honesty, I'd hoped my false bravado would convey to my son that it was now time to move on. But how does a ten year-old comprehend moving on? His only realm of reality is the family unit, and with that destroyed, what does he have left? How does one move beyond loss?

The answer, I suspect, is the same for all of us—time.

Physical wounds result in physical scars—faint reminders of past injuries. Emotional wounds leave no physical sign of hurt. Instead, they chip away pieces of our heart, resulting in the constant need to grieve that which we have lost.

Just as the heartache I experienced from the loss of my father, who I lost over forty-five years ago, my son carries the emotional pain from the dissolution of his family. That loss will always be a reality for him. But what is also a reality is the positive change in our lives that resulted from that loss. My hope is that my son's greatest takeaway from the divorce is that just as change in life is inevitable—and nothing brings about change like divorce—change promotes hope, and hope is always worth fighting for. My sincere wish is that every parent battling the aftermath of divorce embraces that same belief. ♥

CHAPTER FIVE

BRAD

Brad was fourteen when his parents announced their divorce, a decision that challenged the stability of his family and propelled him into the role of caregiver for his two younger brothers, providing Brad a sense of purpose during this time of uncertainty.

❤

Breaking the News

The Larsen boys were gathered in the living room, hovered around the TV, anxiously awaiting the 1992 presidential election results when their parents entered the room.

"Turn the TV down," Greg, Brad's father, instructed, "We need to have a family talk."

Brad did as he was told while his parents moved to the center of the room, blocking the TV.

"I thought we were going to watch the election results," Liam said.

"What we have to say is more important," Greg said, his voice rising in pitch. "Your mother and I are getting a divorce."

The boys remained motionless on the couch, their eyes widening as they looked from one to the other. The only sound in the room was the low whisper of the announcer's voice.

"Bill Clinton has just won the election," Dan Rather reported.

Brad leaned his head down next to his five-year-old brother, Erik. "Do you understand what Dad said?" he asked.

Erik shook his head and then began to cry. Brad wrapped his arm around his shoulder and pulled him close.

"It'll be okay. We'll all be okay," Brad said.

Twelve-year-old Liam turned to Brad with a scowl on his face. "Do you really believe that?" he said, spitting out his words.

The brothers huddled together on the couch—as if trying to keep warm—and watched as their parents turned their backs on them and then left the room.

Once they were gone, Brad tightened his grip on Erik's shoulder. "You've got me, little guy. Always remember that."

Twenty-eight years later, Brad, an IT specialist and ordained minister, recounts his surprise at his parents' announcement.

"I don't remember having had any sense that this was coming. I thought I had the traditional family. Everything was just fine," Brad says. "In that moment basically all those assumptions collapsed. My world just became something different."

Delivering the news of an impending divorce is a daunting task, and Collom admits there is no easy way to brace a child for this type of announcement.

"Hopefully, you have two healthy enough parents that can approach it in a way that's supportive toward the child. Try to stay neutral regarding how they feel about the spouse. Try to make the child understand it's not them. Children, whether we like it or not, they assume it's them," Collom explains.

Long Separations

Over the years, Greg and Lorraine successfully sheltered their children from the animosity they felt toward one another, which triggered an alarming degree of insecurity for Brad when they made their decision to divorce. In addition, his parents' separation, which lasted over a year, signaled the possibility of a reconciliation, adding to the adolescent's state of confusion.

According to licensed marriage and family therapist, Jayne Marsh, who specializes in stepfamilies, long separations "cause the child even more confusion about what's going on."

That was certainly true for Brad, who felt as though he was living in a "limbo-like state." This change in the family dynamic coincided with the start of his freshman year of high school, which made maneuvering this new chapter of his life difficult, especially on his first day of school.

Keeping his head down, Brad traveled the unfamiliar hallways until he heard a familiar voice. He looked up and saw Shane, his friend from middle school.

"Hey, Brad. What's up?" Shane asked.

Brad smiled and waved. "I'm headed to homeroom. I think it's close by," he said.

Shane shook his head. "It's weird, isn't it, not knowing where to go?"

Brad nodded. "Yeah, I know what you mean. Nothing's the same. It's kind of scary," he said, staring at the floor embarrassed by his confession.

"Well, not really scary. Just different, right?" Shane said.

"Sure, different. That's what I meant," Brad said, having to look up at his friend who now towered over him; last year, he was a foot shorter than Brad. So much had changed. Nothing was the same now.

"Hey, man. Are you okay?" Shane asked.

"Sure, I'm fine, just not sure where I'm going," Brad said, forcing a laugh, attempting to hide that this was how he felt about every aspect of his life now.

"I think my room is at the other end," Shane said, just as the bell sounded. "Okay, gotta go," he called out over his shoulder as he headed down the hall.

As the distance grew between them, Brad felt a sudden tightness in his chest, and his throat closed. So much of his life was changing, and all of it was out of his control.

"When will it be normal again?" he whispered under his breath as he shifted his backpack and took a step forward.

Reflecting on that time, Brad rakes his fingers through his auburn hair. "It was tough," he says. "My first year of high school, it was like, is this permanent?"

The Caregiver Role

During this time of uncertainty, Brad's unwavering devotion for his brothers proved a helpful diversion from having to confront his feelings.

"It gave me something to focus on. It gave me something to do. I think that helped," Brad says. "I know I took on a very strong sense of responsibility for them, but I think I may have already had some of that, being the oldest."

Brad's dedication to his brothers never faltered, even when it came to Liam, the most volatile of the three boys.

"Because Liam and I were so close in age, he was always there, so I felt a responsibility for him, but I also needed my space from him," Brad says, shaking his head.

Brad was especially protective of Erik since he felt the young boy had no way of understanding or expressing his feelings.

"It's just all of a sudden his world is upside down, and he's five," Brad says.

The boys' visitation schedules varied due to Greg's work hours and small living space. Brad's parents respected his status as the eldest son and encouraged him to weigh in on the living arrangements.

"We had this alternating schedule where my youngest brother and I moved together," Brad says. "That was one of the things that I specifically voiced. If anyone's going to have someone with him, it's going to be Erik."

Many parents seek equal shared physical custody, as in Brad's case, but according to Scott, that arrangement is not necessarily the best for the child.

"The child is now responsible for remembering everything," Scott says. "Where is my homework? Where is my jacket? They actually become a little parentified themselves in being responsible and not having one location that is theirs. They are told by the courts, or their parents, where they're going and when. Imagine how a child feels."

Support is Essential

Faith played a key role in the story of Greg and Lorraine, Brad's mother, since they first met at a Christian camp. It continued to be an essential aspect of their lives as their family grew, and in turn, had always been an integral part of Brad's life. Years into the marriage, Greg chose to leave the church. Soon after, he left his family. Brad believes if his father had stayed connected to his faith, he would have stayed connected to his family.

"Still, even to this day, I put the bulk of the responsibility on my dad," Brad says. "He's the one who made the decision to leave. He's the one who left."

As a result of his parents' separation, Brad lost the support of his church family as well.

"The church was definitely an important part of our life," Brad says. "It was a part of my life. The divorce itself rocked me immensely, and many at the church didn't seem to know how to handle that. During the separation, the church got very weird about it."

Losing such an essential support system deeply affected Brad, to the point that by his junior year, he considered leaving the church—just like his father. During this same time, a new youth pastor, Pastor Duncan, joined the congregation, and through his guidance, reaffirmed Brad's faith.

"He just got me involved in doing things and helping me feel welcome and me feeling valued," Brad says.

Brad's initial meeting with the young pastor took place one afternoon when a small group of teens gathered outside of the school invited Brad to join their conversation.

"Did you hear about Pastor Duncan?" Jason asked.

"Yeah!" The group broke out in a unanimous cheer at the mention of the young pastor's name.

"He's so cool," Rebecca said, her eyes growing wide.

"He has all kinds of ideas about youth group. I'm excited to see what he does first," Patricia said, adding, "Have you met him yet?"

Brad shook his head, and the teens gasped in unison.

"He's over at the church right now. You've got to meet him," Jason said.

Sweat trickled down Brad's shirt as he walked across the schoolyard in the late summer heat, but once he stepped inside the cool, dark church, an immediate sense of relief washed over him.

Moving down the aisle, Brad wondered just what he'd say to the new pastor, and when he realized he had no idea, he did an about-face and headed for the front door. Before he reached it, he heard an unfamiliar voice call out. "Give me a minute, and I'll be right out."

Brad wiped the palms of his hands on his jeans as the new pastor emerged from the side altar and approached him. He was in his early thirties, with dark hair, a little long in the back, clean-shaven, faded jeans, and a T-shirt. Although his appearance wasn't exactly what Brad expected a pastor to look like, it was his smile that really stood out for Brad.

"Pastor Duncan," he said, extending his hand, adding, "Who do I have the pleasure of meeting?"

Brad stuttered a bit before finding his voice. "I'm Brad Larsen, a junior here at South Side," he said.

"Wonderful. I'm so happy to meet you. I think I met your mother. Lorraine, isn't it?" he said.

Brad looked down at his shoes. "Yes, that's my mom," he said to the floor.

"She seems like a lovely woman, and she shared with me what your family's been going through," he said, adding, "I'm truly sorry."

Brad's head shot up. He couldn't believe his mother would talk about the separation—to anyone. Brad's face flooded with heat, and he quickly turned away.

"I've got to get home. Nice to meet you," Brad said.

Making his way down the aisle, he realized he wasn't alone. Pastor Duncan followed alongside him.

"Brad, please don't be upset," Pastor Duncan said. "I won't say a word about your family to anyone. I think your mom just needed someone to talk to. In fact, if you ever need someone to listen, please know I'm here for you," he said.

Brad turned, expecting a look of pity on the man's face but instead saw a sincere kindness reflected in his eyes—something he'd not received in some time.

"Thank you. I appreciate that," Brad said, realizing he meant it.

On his way home, Brad couldn't shake the image of the smiling pastor, and for a reason he couldn't explain, he felt a sense of calm envelop him.

With a renewed connection in his faith, Brad's future plans changed course. Instead of pursuing a career in architecture as he'd previously considered, Brad felt God was calling him to the world of ministry. He credits Pastor Duncan with providing him the support he needed during this time of transition.

"If he hadn't been there for me, I wouldn't have had that safe place," Brad says. "That pastor saw something in me. He was there right when I needed him to be. If it hadn't been for him, a lot of things in my life wouldn't have played out the way they did."

Support is essential for children of divorce as it enables them to move forward with the healing process during this time of transition. Ideally, parents fill that role, but according to Scott, other people in the child's life may also provide a comforting source.

"Recovering from any trauma in childhood has a lot to do with other people throughout our lives who have been loving toward us, who are modeling loving parental caregiving," Scott says.

Through Pastor Duncan's support, Brad achieved a sense of clarity, realizing that his parents were the same as all human beings—plagued by faults and frailties.

"They were broken, they were hurt, and they were reacting to that," Brad says.

Even in the difficult times, Brad felt his mother was always there for him.

"I know she didn't check out on us," Brad says. "I think for her, her protecting us and making sure we were taken care of just kind of amplified at that time."

Unfortunately, when it came to her relationship with his father, Brad saw a different side to his mother. One instance in particular when she told him, "The man who divorced me was not the same man I met," infused doubt in Brad's mind. His worry that he'd grow up to be just like his father became a constant fear.

Terranova advises parents to keep their opinions to themselves, especially when referencing their ex-spouses, thereby allowing children to draw their own opinions about their parents.

"Even a child at fifteen or sixteen, parents think they're old enough to hear this stuff and really know what's going on, and no, that child needs to make the decision for himself on how they feel about their parent," Terranova says.

The same applies after the divorce. For the child, their parents' continuous bickering is a constant reminder of a painful time in all their lives.

"Divorce is incredibly stressful and difficult, and there are a lot of unresolved issues that come to the surface, and we know the raw spots in our partners. When we are no longer entrusted in that relationship, when that's ended, sometimes it's like all bets are off, and everything that's been unresolved comes out in a very negative way," Scott cautions.

She urges parents to be there for the child as a supportive resource.

"Help them understand what they're experiencing and separate that out from however you're feeling as a parent," she says.

Healthy communication between parents sends an equally powerful message, according to Terranova.

"People can break up, and it doesn't have to mean bad things," she says.

For Brad, his parents' ongoing arguments resulted in a loss of confidence in them both.

"For me, they are not ones I can emotionally rely on, so I'm not going to confide in them when I need someone to be emotionally strong for me," Brad says. "So they're not my emotional safety net. I became aware of the hurts they both harbored and how that shaped the stories they told about themselves and each other."

A Child's Part

Most children assume the blame for their parents' divorce, whereas Brad wondered if there was something he could have done to help save the marriage. The day he arrived home from school and found his father's car in the driveway helped him realize that was never a possibility. Heading inside to see what prompted his father's unexpected visit, Brad opened the front door and was immediately assaulted by a tirade of shouting.

Taking the stairs two at a time, Brad first searched his brother's room. Finding it empty, he continued down the hallway to his mother's bedroom, where he saw his father pacing frantically back and forth while his mother sat perched on the edge of the bed, her head in her hands.

"How many times do I have to tell you, Lorraine, I'm sick and tired of your interfering in my life," Greg shouted.

Lorraine stood up. "I only called about the boys. They're your sons, Greg. The divorce hasn't changed that," she answered.

"It's just an excuse. I know you too well. You've always been this way, and you always will be. Nothing is ever enough for you; you always need more," Greg shouted.

Their faces flushed and fists clenched, Brad wondered to himself, *who are these people*? He'd never seen his parents this angry.

"Do you know what I did the day of our divorce? I threw a party. I was so happy to be rid of you," Greg said, a sneer spreading across his face as he glared at his ex-wife.

Lorraine sat down on the bed, threw her head back, then released a menacing laugh.

"You think I care?" she said. "All the years we've been together, nothing was more important than your work, not even your children. I'm happy to be rid of you."

She stood up, reached out, and shoved Greg in the chest. "You'll be lucky if your sons ever want to see you again," she said.

"Mom!" Brad called from the doorway, unable to keep silent.

His mother rushed across the room and grabbed him by the shoulders. "You should never have seen this. I'm so, so, sorry," she said.

Brad stared at his parents—his father, standing silent and still, and his mother, crumpled on the floor in tears. He turned away from them both, ran to his room, closed the door, and started to pray.

Moving On

By the time Brad was in college, his father had accepted a job out of state, which resulted in Lorraine being awarded full custody of Erik, who at the time was a freshman in high school. His father's decision reinforced for Brad that when it came down to it, his father always put himself first.

"It was him and then the rest of us," Brad says. "I can only imagine what that said to my youngest brother. He's definitely been an influence on me, but not as a mentor. He's one that projects his impression of you. If your opinion doesn't agree with his, you're wrong."

His parents' divorce deeply shook Brad's belief in the security of his family, and this uncertainty remained with him into adulthood, causing him serious doubts regarding marriage.

"I wanted to get married, but I was terrified of the prospect," Brad says.

According to Scott, past hurts carried into adulthood many times factor into a person's choice for a relationship, seeking those who also have a hurt they are trying to heal.

"If we don't work through [the relationship], it doesn't end up working because we're following the same pattern," Scott says. "We absorb whatever happens in our family. It becomes a part of us."

Over eighteen years ago, Brad took a chance on love when he met the woman he considers his greatest source of support, his wife Stephanie. It's his belief that God led him to her, and he is forever grateful for her presence in his life.

Continuing his efforts to lend support where it's needed, Brad regularly volunteers at local organizations where he offers both spiritual and physical help, especially to the children. Giving to those in need defined the man Brad is today.

"For me, a person is valuable not because of what they can do, but for who they are," Brad says. "My ideal world is where everyone shows and expresses their love for one another and helps one another."

My Thoughts

A positive role model is an immeasurable asset in all children's lives. For a child of divorce, it is even more so. That person, whether it be a pastor, priest, teacher, or neighbor, provides hope during a time of uncertainty. Unlike Brad, my son didn't have anyone like that in his life. He'd always counted on his parents for guidance. The divorce destroyed his trust in the family, his trust in us as parents, just as it did for Brad, and as an only child, he never felt more alone.

My attempts to provide him help through group counseling sessions proved futile. His lack of participation was proof to the counselors—and to me—that was not the help he wanted. So once again, he was on his own, traveling a path of uncertainty, distancing himself from the people he normally would have turned to for help because we had let him down.

Over the years, through conversations with my son, he shared what it was he needed during this difficult time, a time he describes as "feeling like the earth cracked in two." Never, in all of our talks, did his father or I ask him what *he* needed. Such a simple question, and yet how many parents have the insight to ask? I know I didn't. As it turns out, that's exactly what he was searching for, the opportunity to provide input instead of simply being an observer in the chaos of what was now his world.

According to the experts, the loss of control is one of the most difficult concepts for children to deal with following their parents' divorce or separation. As parents, we need to be aware of how important it is to our child to feel they're as much a part of the reshaping of the family and a valued participant in the multitude of ongoing changes, as we are. They need to know their voice is heard. I was unable to provide this resource to my son, which would have allowed him the opportunity to feel included, not separated, from the people he loved most in this world. ❤

CHAPTER SIX

NOAH

Noah, husband, father, and published author, was nine years old when his parents divorced. Their decision of joint physical custody of Noah and his younger sister resulted in the children shuffling from one home to another on a weekly basis. This unstructured lifestyle, coupled with his mother's unpredictable parenting style, produced a lack of stability in Noah's life, which still affects him today.

♥

A New Home

Noah's mother, Irene, held the door open to her new two-bedroom apartment as she ushered her children inside.

"Well, what do you think?" she said, waving her hand through the air, doing her best Vanna White impression.

"I know it needs some work: curtains, a nice throw rug, and some artwork on the walls, but don't you just love it?" she asked with exaggerated excitement.

Noah watched his mother parade around the cramped space—taking four steps from the living room to the kitchen—while Melissa, his three-year-old sister, plopped down on the floor and began sucking her thumb.

"So, where do we sleep?" Noah asked.

Irene turned away from the kitchen and focused on her children. "It's just down the hall. Let's go take a look," she said, prompting the children to follow her.

Once inside the small room, she opened the blinds. The late afternoon sun streamed through the small window and landed on an ugly brown stain in the middle of the carpeted floor.

"What's that?" Noah said, pointing at the spot. "It looks like poop."

Irene's laugh caught in her throat.

"I'm sure it's just a soda stain. Nothing to worry about," she said. "Your beds will go on either side of the room, and I'll get new comforters for you both. Doesn't that sound great?"

"So, we have to share a room?" Noah said, shaking his head as he started to walk out.

Irene caught up with him at the door. "Where do you think you're going?" she said. "This is your weekend with me. We can have a moving in party. I made a cake."

Noah took a quick look around, grimaced, and then called to his sister, "Melissa, time to go. Mom's taking us back to Dad's house," he said before heading out the door.

Now in his late forties, Noah lowers his six-foot-four frame into a chair, leans back, and takes a sip of his coffee. Speaking about his family home, his tone is almost mournful, as he explains it was sold out of necessity after the divorce.

"I still think about that house. I wish we still had it," Noah says. "I think on some level, I've always sort of regretted that, and maybe my dad has too."

The sale of the family home initiated the beginning of a transient lifestyle for Noah.

"Once we left there, I started hopping around from one school to another," he says, adding, "I made twenty moves in twenty-one years. That was really unsettling."

For children of divorce, the loss of the family home is an additional adjustment to an already unstable situation. Shannon suggests maintaining daily routines as a way to minimize a child's stress during this time.

"Have similar structure in both households so the kid has less transitions," Shannon suggests.

Personality Changes

As a way of providing a semblance of normalcy for his son, who had always been a very positive child, Murray, Noah's father, a professor of anthropology, moved to an apartment in Noah's school district.

"I was kind of like this person who would wake up happy every day, and my natural state of things was just happiness," Noah says.

After the move, that was no longer the case.

"I was really starting to act out and be upset and get angry at school," Noah says.

Fortunately his fifth-grade teacher provided the support he needed.

"The teacher, she'd given me this sign and I could just leave the classroom if I was getting really angry at something," Noah explained. "I'd leave and just walk around a little. She was helping me manage my anger."

Noah now views his acting out as an expression of his frustration at the time. Collom's explanation confirms his theory that anger is many times a child's first behavioral response to divorce.

"They get aggressive with their toys, two dolls fighting, cars crashing. They play it out through those things," Collom says, adding some might be drawn to play with matches.

"Fire is a reflection of being angry inside, burning inside, wanting to destroy things," Collom says.

Minerva suggests that in the case of a separation or divorce, parents notify teachers and those with regular contact with their child and make them aware of what's happening at home.

"Ask for feedback, problems in the classroom, or if they see issues," Minerva says. "Let them know *you* want to know because kids don't have language to express that stuff. It's going to happen behaviorally."

Therapy—Not Always the Answer

In an attempt to help their son adjust to the new family dynamic, Noah's parents arranged for him to see a therapist. On the initial visit Irene, a therapist herself, accompanied Noah.

"Don't be nervous. Dr. Knox is a very nice man. You'll like him," she said, patting his hand lightly.

Noah moved his hand away and turned his attention to the large aquarium on the far wall—the rhythmic movements of the fish proving to be more soothing than his mother's touch. Moments later, the office door opened and a tall man in his late fifties, dressed in gray slacks and a white dress shirt, stepped into the lobby.

"Noah Blankenship," he announced.

Irene gave her son a slight nudge. "The doctor is calling you," she said.

Noah remained fixated on the fish, so Irene nudged him again.

"Go on. It'll be fine. I'll be here when you finish," she said, showcasing a nervous smile.

The young boy walked toward the man he was there to see—not really understanding why he had to see him. He was a doctor. Noah wasn't sick. So why was he here?

"Why don't we step inside my office," Dr. Knox said, opening the door.

Forty-five minutes later, the boy exited the office and joined his mother.

"How was your talk with Dr. Knox?" she asked, her smile strained.

Looking back at the room he'd just exited, Noah smiled.

"He's got a lot of cool toys," he said. "I built houses out of Lincoln logs, and then I *smashed* them all up with big metal bolts. Dr. Knox said I can play with them some more next week. Can we go now?"

Over the next two years, Noah alternated between sessions with Dr. Knox and one other therapist, but he feels neither provided much support.

"I was pretty opposed to it all along, I never liked it, and I really don't remember talking to those people," he says.

Experts agree that counseling can prove beneficial, but Scott points out the fact that not every child needs it.

"They may not be in a place where they even want to process it. They may not want to understand it. Sometimes you have to wait. Ask the child," Scott says, adding, instead of sending the child for professional help, the parent should consider going instead.

"I would say the parent get some kind of counseling and start talking about what's happening," Scott says.

Terranova agrees. When a child understands their parents have resources available to help them, it often alleviates their feeling of responsibility regarding their welfare.

"Good therapy can help because you can get some distance and some perspective," Terranova says. "I would want any parent to say this is not on your shoulders, and I actually have resources to handle this. I can still be a parent here, and I got this."

Joint Custody, Not Always the Best Choice

The decision to have their children spend equal time with each parent led to a transient lifestyle for Noah and his sister, which instilled a constant state of instability in the young boy.

"It was very peripatetic, living out of a suitcase or a duffel bag," Noah says. "We'd go to my mom's on Thursday night, and then Friday night, and sometimes on Saturday night. We'd go there on Monday afternoons."

As adversarial as it may sound, shared physical custody might not always be the best choice. Scott questions its benefits.

"It's really an interesting shift in our culture that we've moved to, this place where the general feeling is that fifty-fifty is the best thing for everybody, and I'm not so sure that is actually true for the child," Scott says. "The parenting that happens in these two locations is usually completely different."

The only stability in Noah's life during this time of transition was Melissa, his sister, who made the weekly moves with him.

"We sort of had each other as constants in our lives. We were walking the same path, but we weren't always connecting," Noah says. "At the time, it didn't really register or mean anything to us. When I look back on it, it seems significant."

Noah realizes now that Melissa's behavior reflected obvious signs that even at the age of three, she was impacted by their parents' divorce.

"She had this method of coping where she'd just put her thumb in her mouth and get this glassy look on her face," Noah explains. "She had a blanket that she'd touch with her fingers and suck her thumb and zone out. I know she sucked her thumb for a really long time, until she was in sixth grade."

Adjusting to his parents' lifestyles from week to week added to Noah's feelings of insecurity. Irene's carefree style was the direct opposite of Murray's, who mandated strict rules and restrictions in his home.

"I wasn't a huge fan of him in those days, probably because he was stricter than my mom," Noah says.

One of the advantages of staying at his mother's was that Noah felt like he was living an alternate reality.

"I thought that was cool that I had access to something else," Noah says. "I had different toys at my mom's. I had like video games and computer games, and I could watch TV, and I liked those things."

A Turning Point

As much as he enjoyed his mother's loose reign, Irene's unstable parenting forced Noah to handle responsibilities far beyond his abilities. One afternoon, while in the front seat of his mother's Ford Fairlane, Noah watched as Irene jammed a cooler, towels, and pool toys into the trunk of her car and then slammed it shut.

She then checked on Melissa, who sat quietly sucking her thumb in the back seat. Noah tuned the radio to his favorite rock station, KNVX, and gave his mother a disgruntled look as she took her seat behind the wheel.

"It's already one o'clock. We should have been at the pool by now," he said. "Why does it always take you so long to do everything?"

Irene turned away from her son, her eyes swelling with tears, clamped both hands on the steering wheel, slammed the car in reverse, then hit the gas. A moment later a loud *bang* reverberated throughout the car, quickly followed by a sharp, metallic, scraping noise.

Irene jammed on the breaks and checked the rear-view mirror. The back seat passenger door—which she'd forgotten to close—was crumpled like an accordion and wedged behind a telephone pole. Slamming the car in park, Irene jumped out of the car, screaming and cursing.

Noah did a quick check on his sister, who sat silent and stared into space, then jumped out and ran around the car. He stopped short when he found his mother lying flat on the ground, stomping her feet. Soon, passersby gathered, forming a semi-circle around the middle-aged woman demonstrating a full-blown tantrum for all to see. Feeling a rush of heat rise to his face, Noah stared at the madwoman on the ground and realized he had no idea what to do.

"I was standing there thinking, *I don't know how the fuck to deal with this,*" Noah says as he slams his fist on the table. He says his mother was never the same after that.

"She started to prioritize her own needs over mine," Noah says. "She was having so much trouble managing what she needed to manage that I sort of had to become the parent."

Unaware that his mother was suffering from bipolar disorder and depression, Noah was confused by her self-obsessed attitude. The fact that she needed him to step in and take control in situations far beyond his comprehension proved to be an emotionally jarring experience for the young boy.

"It's like a weight on your shoulders. It's like you have to support your parent, and you're not ready for that. I just felt like I had to do something, and I don't think I always knew how or what to do," Noah says. "I had real needs as a kid at that age, and so for her not to be able to meet those needs felt like a betrayal. I feel like I'm still trying to find acceptance as a result of missing that growing up."

Terranova explains that the term parentification is used for this type of behavior—transferring the parental role to the child—which many times results in stunting the emotional and developmental growth of the child. In addition, this behavior may hinder a child's self-identity and independence.

"On the other hand, it may cause that child to become a type A person who is task-oriented in everything they do because they weren't allowed to have the time to play because of the adult responsibilities that were thrust on them," Terranova says. "The playfulness of life was sort of a non-value."

Choosing to Disconnect

As unsettling as his life with Irene was, living with his father presented its own set of challenges. Murray's insistence that his children attend the best schools prompted numerous moves, which began in sixth grade for Noah, and continued through his high school years. This resulted in positioning Noah in the role of the new kid, time and again.

The location of the schools posed additional challenges. Growing up in an inner-city neighborhood on the East Coast, Noah's first move relocated him to the suburbs, where he felt he never really fit in.

"I'd grown up in the south end, a lot of ethnic diversity, and that really was part of my identity," Noah says.

A year and another school later, Noah returned to a more urban environment, which provided him a sense of familiarity. Unfortunately, by ninth grade, Murray moved once more back to the suburbs.

"It was just not a good situation," Noah says. "It seemed like a lot of the kids in that town had lived their whole lives there, and so they really knew each other long term. It was just a very different kind of ethos than what I was used to. It was very different."

Rather than try and adjust, Noah distanced himself, denying himself the opportunity to establish new friendships.

"I was pretty burnt out on being the new kid and building relationships so I just kind of kept to myself," Noah says, adding he chose to spend his lunchtime at home rather than "try to figure out who to sit with in the cafeteria."

Noah chose to live at his mother's during his high school years as it allowed him to be near his friends and girlfriend—a choice that strengthened his feeling of disconnectedness from his high school environment.

"It was kind of like having two different lives, never really fully assimilating or involving myself in that world of high school," Noah says. "Because I would go away all the time and not really hang out with people there. I sort of just removed myself from the situation to some extent. I was very tentative, and I didn't really step out, or show up, because I'd done that in other situations, and I didn't feel like expelling that energy. I thought being around people would be harder. I wound up spending a lot of time by myself."

Noah still found a way to distance himself in the one aspect of high school he did enjoy—sports. "I didn't really socialize with the players after school. I didn't socialize with them outside of practice, until maybe junior or senior year," he says.

In addition to his disconnectedness, Noah's choice to live with his mother presented the same problems he faced when he was younger, inciting anger and resentment.

"She just wouldn't be in control, so I had to try and get things in control," Noah says. "I wasn't happy with that. And I would treat her badly, and she would just put up with it. Even my friends asked me how could I treat my mom that way?"

Not until years after the divorce did Murray explain to Noah about his mother's bi-polar disorder, admitting it played a major part in the divorce. With a true understanding of his parents' situation, Noah realized his father had always been the stabilizing force in his life.

"He kind of kept things on track," Noah says. "He made sure I was going to school, and I was doing my homework and made sure I was invested, and I was getting good grades."

Divorce Leads to an Epiphany

Noah held off marrying until his late twenties in an attempt to keep from making the same mistakes as his parents. Unfortunately, five years later, his wife filed for divorce, claiming she was in love with another man. Her announcement came as no surprise to Noah, as by that point he considered their relationship unsalvageable.

Throughout his marriage, the idea of starting a family was never a consideration. "I just felt like I wasn't ready, and if I wasn't ready, I wouldn't do it," Noah says.

After the divorce, Noah reflected on his choice and realized that, in fact, he had a sincere desire to be a father.

"I realized I *did* want to have a kid because that was the thing I was mourning," Noah says.

When Noah moved on to his next relationship with his longtime friend and co-worker, Gretchen, they discovered they each shared the desire to start a family. In their third year together, the couple welcomed their daughter, Willow, into the family. Willow's birth was a true revelation to Noah, who happily exclaims fatherhood is "absolutely one of my favorite things."

Noah's initiation into fatherhood had an additional benefit—it strengthened his relationship with Murray. Although Noah admits he and Murray are very different people, he now looks to his father as a role model.

"My dad loves in a different way than other people do, but he's a really good listener, and he's really present and caring," Noah says.

As for his mother, unfortunately, not much has changed.

"In many ways, I'm still supporting her now. It's like I'm responsible for two kids," Noah says. "She literally parallels my daughter in many ways. There's anger around that, yeah."

Noah joined a local men's support group in an effort to work through his anger issues. "Most of the work that I've done there has been around my mom and that period," Noah says as he shakes his head and smiles.

As for his marriage, Noah and Gretchen make a conscious effort to ensure the stability of their relationship by attending regular counseling sessions.

"I really want us to stay together because I want my daughter to have two parents, together, who get along," Noah says. "If my wife and I were going to break up, I honestly would have no idea how to handle it. I really just want to avoid that."

Noah's craft as a writer has been beneficial in helping him work through his feelings regarding his past. Two of his short stories, one written from a divorced father's point of view, and the second from a divorced mother's perspective, provided Noah a better understanding of what his parents went through, and not just how it affected him.

"Those stories helped me sort of envision what these things were like for my mother and father," Noah says. "Going through the whole story of it helps to kind of bridge the present with the past, and I feel more comfortable with the way things are."

My Thoughts

Parents want the very best for their children. Divorced parents struggle to achieve that primary goal. Murray was determined to provide the best education for both Noah and Melissa, and as genuine and heartfelt as his intention was, his pursuit resulted in a long period of instability and isolation in his son's life.

A parent's good intentions often fall short amid a divorce, or in the aftermath of one. After my divorce, I was determined to maintain a sense of normalcy in my son's life, and in pursuit of that goal, I began establishing new routines, if not to replace, then at least to make up for those we'd lost. In hindsight, I realized what my son was missing was consistency in his life. Dysfunctional had become his normal.

Even though the new routines and rituals offered a more stable environment, it lacked familiarity. In my mad rush to achieve a semblance of normalcy, subconsciously, I believe I was attempting to erase a great deal of the past. But by erasing the past, I was erasing the first ten years of my son's life. Although that was never my intention, that's how it felt to my son. Focusing on the end goal negated my primary goal of establishing a better life for us both. Over time I learned to slow down, talk to my son, and really listen to what he wanted and needed. Eventually, we arrived at our new normal, and although it wasn't perfect, it felt like a true accomplishment, because we'd built it together. ❤

CHAPTER SEVEN

KATNISS

Katniss is not only a successful businesswoman, entrepreneur, mother, and wife, she is a warrior—just as the character whose name she chose to represent her. In addition to being a child of divorce, Katniss was a victim of parental abuse, as was her younger brother. As the eldest sibling, she willingly accepted the role of caretaker, which established an inseparable bond between the two that continues today.

An Unexplained Event

Katniss woke suddenly when she felt a hand on her shoulder and looked up to find a face peering down at her.

"Mom, what time is it?" she said as she rubbed her eyes.

Sylvie, her mother, pointed to her brother's bed. "Come with me. We need to wake Chris," she said as she crossed the room.

Scrambling out of the covers, Katniss swung her feet off the bed—the tiled floor sending shivers up her spine. Reaching for the fleece blanket, she wrapped it around her threadbare pajamas.

"Time to get up, Chris," Sylvie said to her son.

Grabbing him by the hand, she pulled Chris out of bed and then left the room.

"I guess we're supposed to follow her," Katniss said, her face puffy from sleep.

Taking her brother's hand, she pulled him to the tiny kitchen where they found their mother standing behind an ironing board. An assortment of pills in a variety of colors were laid out on its surface. The children watched as their mother gathered the pills in her hand and then dumped them into her son's hand.

Then she did the same with Katniss, who wrinkled her nose as the pile of pink, blue, and yellow tablets smeared together in her sweaty palm. Hoping for an explanation of what was going on, Katniss instead was handed a cup of water.

"You need to take your medicine," Sylvie said. "You first."

The little girl stared at the pills. "This is a lot of medicine, Mom. Why so much?" she asked, as she dumped the pile into her mouth and took a drink.

"Now your brother," Sylvie instructed.

Chris mimicked his sister's actions, and when he'd finished, flashed his mother a big smile.

"I took them all. I'm a good boy, right?" he said.

Sylvie led her children in a silent march to their bedroom. Then with great care, she tucked them into their beds, pulled up the covers, and turned off the light. As she closed the door, she whispered, "Time to sleep."

As her footsteps echoed down the hallway, Chris whispered to his sister. "Are we supposed to go back to sleep now?"

Katniss sat up and peered across the room. "I think so. I'm feeling pretty tired. We'll ask Mom what this was about in the morning."

Now in her forties, Katniss's appearance exudes the consummate professional: tailored suit, flawless make-up, and not a hair out of place. Sitting tall in her chair, she recalls the haunting incident that took place over three decades ago following her father Roland's threat to leave the family. The cynical tone of her voice hints at the bitterness that remains from that long-ago event.

"She freaked out, I guess, and called an ambulance because my brother started having convulsions, and he was in a comma for several days," Katniss says, explaining what followed that night. "We were put in the hospital, and when I woke up, and I told my dad, he one hundred percent believed me. I'm not sure if she said something to him or had threatened before, but he never questioned it. It was the doctor that was so upset I would say something like that because he'd known her many, many years. We talked about it years later, and my dad thought that she had intended on killing us and maybe freaked out and called the ambulance."

"I think my mom was intentionally trying to make my dad stay, or scare him, or whatever," Katniss says, with a wave of her hand. "He ended up not leaving. They never pressed charges against my mom. So the story was that we had gotten into the stuff."

This level of abuse is certainly extreme, and the majority of children of divorce never experience this type of behavior. Unfortunately, that is not the case with Katniss and her brother. Shannon, who also serves as a child custody evaluator, and provides court-involved therapy in child custody issues and domestic violence, is familiar with this type of situation.

"I think it's about one percent of the population that get divorced that are highly litigious and highly conflictual. It's such a minute population, but I think it's growing," Shannon says, adding, the latest studies suggest that abuse is equal for both men and women.

"When it's a highly conflicted family or any type of abuse, those children are the ones that do not want to see their parents get back together," she adds.

Katniss certainly agrees, although growing up, she was unaware of the severity of their situation and considered their upbringing normal.

"Our parents were very immature, and they were very selfish," Katniss says. "We struggled pretty much all of our lives having not really much of anything. We would go without electricity. We'd been evicted several times because we could not afford to keep things going. We struggled certainly. It was very obvious that there were things that were going on with them, but we didn't necessarily know, because it was regular life. It wasn't out of the ordinary for us. But looking back at it, I can see what it was now," Katniss says.

Everything Changes

Roland's decision to stay was temporary, and Katniss recalls she was in second grade when he left for good. "I remember crying and asking a bunch of questions, but I don't remember what they were and not really understanding why he was leaving," she says. "I know he left with a bunch of trash bags full of clothes, and we stayed in the apartment with my mom."

According to Shannon, children look to their parents' marriage as their role model for relationships, and if they grow up in a dysfunctional one, that's the family model they'll accept as normal. When that level of normal changes, it can be overwhelming for the child, which is what happened the day after Roland left.

Katniss woke to an unaccustomed stillness in the home. She grabbed a pair of jeans and a t-shirt from the heap of dirty clothes on the floor and headed to the living room where she found Chris staring at the TV—a bowl of cereal in one hand, and the remote in the other. When she reached the kitchen, she discovered two half-filled glasses of red wine on the counter—her father's favorite drink.

As her heart pounded against her ribs, she raced to her parents' bedroom. When she got there, the door was closed, and although the rule was to never enter before knocking, excitement overruled her fear, and Katniss burst into the room. Finding her mother still in bed came as no surprise—what did surprise the eight-year-old was the strange man lying beside her.

"You know you should knock," Sylvie said as she pulled the blanket over them both.

"I saw the wine glasses and thought Dad was home," Katniss said, her eyes focused on the stranger.

"Your father has moved on. He's not coming back. You better get used to it," Sylvie said as she leaned over, kissed the man, and then shooed her daughter out of the room with the wave of her hand.

Katniss closed the door, leaned against it, and slowly lowered herself to the floor, the sounds of her mother's laughter echoing in her ears.

"It was like this horrible, horrible moment of not really understanding what was going on," Katniss says with a catch in her throat.

According to Terranova, abandonment is the most universal feeling experienced by children of divorce. But Katniss never had the opportunity to express her feelings to *anyone*, thus denying her an outlet that would aid her in adjusting to the family's new dynamic.

"The more parents are communicating or allowing the child to process things in a healthier manner, given permission to feel their feelings, talk about their feelings without being shut down, the healthier the atmosphere is for people to really show up and process and work through their feelings," Terranova says.

Parents always need to keep in mind that in the midst of so much change, one of a child's greatest needs is to simply be heard.

An Abrupt Move

Not long after the divorce, Sylvie delegated the children's care to Roland when she chose to move to an adults-only apartment.

"From what little I remember, our mom dropped us off at my dad's. She was trying to live this single life. My mom was so selfish. She didn't want to be a parent anymore," Katniss says.

Adjusting to life with her father, who spent the majority of his time with his girlfriend, was not an easy process. On one of his unexpected appearances, Roland announced his arrival by bursting through the front door.

"Where's my guitar?" he shouted.

Katniss turned away from the stove and stared in disgust at her father's faded Metallica T-shirt and ripped jeans.

"It's wherever you left it, Dad," she said, adding, "Maybe you should think about cleaning up."

Roland pointed to his chest. "I'll have you know, *this* is one of my best shirts," he said before heading down the hallway.

A few moments later, he called out, "Found it."

After giving the pot a quick stir, Katniss poured the water and ketchup combo—what passed for tomato soup at their father's house—into a bowl and called for her brother. When Roland returned to the kitchen, guitar in hand, Chris was trailing behind him, the six-year-old's arms wrapped around his father's waist. "Daddy's home," Chris said, adding, "Are you going to eat dinner with us?"

Roland uncurled Chris's arms from his body and then opened the door. Katniss stared at her father, her hands on her hips.

"You can't leave before you give me some money. I need to buy food," she said.

Roland patted down his pockets, then shook his head. "Sorry, haven't got any cash on me. But I know my little girl. You'll make do with what we got," he said as he turned his back to her.

"Gotta go. The gigs two hours away, so I probably won't be back until tomorrow," he added before heading out the door.

Katniss dropped the pot onto the table, red spots splattering its surface, then rushed over and grabbed him by the arm.

"You can't keep leaving us alone," she said with a quiver in her voice. "We have no money, and we're nearly out of food."

Katniss pointed to Chris, who'd taken a seat at the table. "Your kids are eating ketchup water. What is wrong with you?" she said, tears streaking her cheeks, unable to hold back her frustration.

Roland simply shrugged his shoulders. "You know how much my music means to me," he said. "Someday I'll make it big, and then we'll live in a palace. You'll see," he added as he shut the door behind him.

Katniss wipes at the corner of her eye, then releases an audible sigh.

"He's been in a band since I could breathe," she says. "He's always had this crazy rock star mentality and lived that lifestyle while we were home by ourselves. I just remember it being me and my brother. I am the oldest, and I kind of took that responsibility. I was very much a protector of him. It's made us very close."

Possibly the only advantage Katniss had growing up was that she was not an only child, according to Minerva. "When there are siblings, and they have the ability to connect to each other, even if they haven't really communicated explicitly about what's going on, there is at least a sense that there is someone else going through it with them," Minerva says. "They're not going through it alone."

Katniss agrees and believes she drew strength from looking after her brother. "I think because he was there, I was probably stronger—I had more of a fight," she says.

A Chance to Escape

As much as she coveted her role as caregiver, when an opportunity to relinquish that role presented itself—even if only for a few weeks—Katniss took advantage of it. When she was twelve, she attended a church summer camp, and on the last day, she sat waiting in the counselor's office for her dad to pick her up. Hearing a car pull in the driveway, she ran to the window and looked out. Expecting to see her father's Grand Am, she was surprised to find her mother's Ford parked in the driveway.

"Your dad took Chris on a fishing trip," Sylvie explained as Katniss got in the passenger seat. "You'll be staying with me for a few days while they're gone."

A week later, with Roland still a no-show, Katniss decided it was time for some answers.

"So when am I going back to Dad's?" Katniss asked as she took a seat on her mother's bed. "I thought he was only going to be gone for a few days."

Sylvie looked up from her magazine, then tossed it aside.

"Okay, time for the truth," she said. "Your dad wasn't on a fishing trip. He just doesn't want you living with him anymore," she said, adding, "Could you close the door behind you. I have a lot of reading to do."

Katniss felt her heart skip a beat, uncertain if it was from relief or disappointment. "What about Chris? Is he staying here too?" she asked.

"No," Sylvie said, adding with a smirk, "I guess your father likes him."

Katniss closed the bedroom door and then walked the darkened hallway to her room. She'd never felt so alone.

"Now my brother and I are split up, and he had this whole other upbringing that I was not a part of," Katniss says. Initially, she resented Chris because her father chose him over her.

"Although, I still felt protective of him," Katniss says. "For the most part, when it mattered most, we were a team. I remember it more when we were living with my dad, being alone and feeling like I had to protect him. There was a different dynamic as we got older."

Siblings Reunited

In her freshman year of high school, Katniss was reunited with her brother. Roland's ex-wife, who he married soon after the divorce, dropped Chris off at Sylvie's door using the excuse she couldn't handle him anymore. As happy as the siblings were to be back together, the reunion alone couldn't offset the emotional toll each had experienced by that point in their lives. When once again, Sylvie left them on their own for the night, Chris could no longer hold back his anger.

"She's just like Dad. Neither of them cares about me—they never have," he said, his face turning crimson as he slammed his fists on the bed.

"Well, you're not alone little brother. They don't care about me, either," Katniss said, taking a seat beside him.

Chris lowered his head into his hands, and Katniss watched as his body shook uncontrollably. Tears sprung to her eyes, and a moment later, she jumped up and bolted to the bathroom, returning with a large bottle of aspirin, which she opened and poured into her mouth.

Chris watched in horror and then reached out and grabbed the bottle from her hands. "No, you can't leave me. I won't let you," he shouted.

A deadly game of tug-of-war ensued, ending with Chris in possession of the bottle. "Well, if you're not staying here, neither am I," he said, putting the bottle to his mouth and leaning his head back.

As Katniss watched the pills spill into her brother's mouth, she flashed back to the aftermath of her mother's unsuccessful overdose attempt years ago. Chris lying in the hospital bed, his face ghostly white and unnaturally still. Waiting for him to wake from his coma were the longest days of her life.

Blinking back her tears, Katniss quickly reached out, grabbed his hand, and then pulled him into the bathroom. Filling a cup with water, she shoved it at him. "Drink this," she said.

Countless cups later, Chris leaned over and vomited in the bathtub, tiny remnants of the aspirin lining the bottom of the porcelain tub. Fearing that wasn't enough, Katniss grabbed Chris and attempted a maneuver she'd learned at school called the Heimlich. Afterward, bloated and exhausted, the children lay on the bathroom floor as Katniss prayed for their lives to be spared.

Shaking her head and blotting her eyes, it's obvious the memory is still a painful one for Katniss.

"I remember waking up after vomiting all night and thinking, 'Oh my gosh, we're still alive," she says, adding, "I think that we are obviously a product of the divorce, but I really believe that all of the other stuff that they did had more of an effect on who we are."

Then she pauses, cocks her head, and adds. "It's a culmination of the two, I suppose." It's a conversation she and her brother have all the time—how they managed to survive such a dysfunctional upbringing.

"We've maintained a pretty close relationship. I think it will always be that way. It really was just us against the world. We've come a long way, which is amazing," she says with a smile.

Moving On

Even after Chris arrived, living with Sylvie proved problematic for Katniss. By the time she was sixteen, she had moved out for good, which resulted in a transient lifestyle for the teen.

"I bounced around to different places until I graduated," Katniss says, and only agreed to return home after her mother completed rehab.

"So I moved back for a couple of months when I was eighteen or so, to help with her, and then it blew up again, and I just left," Katniss explains.

The two remained estranged until Katniss was in college and planning her wedding to her college sweetheart. Their reunion was brief.

"She didn't show up to the wedding. She didn't even call," Katniss says. "When I finally got her she gave me the excuse that she was sick, which was pretty much the last straw. It left a very bitter taste in my mouth and didn't exactly start our marriage off great either."

Her marriage never recovered from its rocky start, and a year later, the couple divorced. Katniss attributes her relationship failures to her past and believes the same can be said for Chris.

"I think we both had deficiencies in relationships because we didn't get the stuff we needed when we were young," Katniss says. "And I think that's been a struggle for me personally in my relationships, feeling a sense of trust, and being able to let go and truly be one hundred percent in the relationship. I was always half way in. In case it hit the fan, I wasn't going to be the one holding the bag."

"When you have parents that are so selfish and treat you so poorly, you have to wonder—if they can't love you, who can? So going into a relationship feeling that way, you're never going to survive the relationship. I had no frame of reference for what love was."

Motherhood

Soon after her divorce, Katniss discovered she was pregnant with her son, Ryan. She reunited briefly with her ex but soon realized having a child was certainly no cure for a bad relationship. Ryan's birth resulted in an epiphany for Katniss.

"I understood for the first time that there was nothing he could ever do that I would walk away," Katniss says. "And I certainly didn't feel that with anyone before."

She has no regrets regarding her divorce and believes it was the best choice for her and for Ryan. "Instead of having just the one family as a role model, he has two—which he's immersed in. And I think that's better."

Surprisingly, Katniss has no regrets about her childhood and credits her past with providing her the strength that allowed her to not only survive, but thrive.

"When I feel down about anything, I think about that, and it kind of gives me that positive feeling of accomplishment," Katniss says. "It makes me appreciate where I am."

Scott certainly agrees and believes an essential key to happiness is the ability to let go of your past and focus on the future.

"Whatever happened to you when you were children is done; it's over. You can't change it. I think that's the thing that's really important to let people know," Scott says. "We can heal from it and do things differently. We can't change the temperament of somebody, but we can gain coping mechanisms to help us. That's what we all do. That's how we live in the world."

My Thoughts

For the first decade of my son's life, I allowed my ex-husband to dominate our family through his use of physical and mental abuse, subjecting my son to a father whose anger could escalate to a threatening degree. I have very little memory of the worst of those times, and I credit my lapse of memory to self-preservation.

I do remember making the decision to end the cycle of dysfunctionality by ending the marriage because my fear of what would happen to my son if we stayed far outweighed all other fears. Armed with the certainty that I'd made the best decision for my son and me, I was able to withstand the painful months that followed.

Experts agree, finding themselves thrust into a new family dynamic, a child must find a way to express their feelings to the myriad of changes taking place in their lives, too many of which they have no say. My son made it painfully clear that he was feeling anger. He was equally clear that he blamed me for his anger, as I destroyed our family.

You can imagine my relief when a professional therapist explained that a child of divorce many times vents their anger at the parent who they are assured will always offer them unconditional love. Although this fact eased my conscience, the heartache of my son's accusations didn't suddenly dissipate. Understanding his need to label me the villain—as directing his anger toward his father was not an option—I was able to accept his accusations, knowing that was a part of his healing. My son, like all children of divorce, had to transition through his anger to reach acceptance, although I was uncertain how long that journey would take.

As we ventured through the rocky path to our new life, I drew comfort from my faith in my son and my faith in God, praying every night for his anger to ease, for his "I love you's" to return. I waited for nine months. When the moment came, and he uttered those three words, I knew my son was back. Surpassing this major hurdle in creating a new life together provided me with the confidence to continue our journey. Although I wasn't so naive to think this would be our only challenge, (and it certainly wasn't), the fact that we survived was enough. After all, we had survived much worse. Our future was still unclear, and as unsettling as that was, the knowledge that we would make those steps together filled me with hope, and I found that was enough. ❤

CHAPTER EIGHT

CHRIS

Despite being subjected to parents who were either too selfish or too immature to provide a stable home environment, Chris, is happily married, a proud father, and a successful entrepreneur—proof of his prevailing fortitude. In addition to abandonment issues brought on by his parents' divorce when he was six, Chris developed an overly sensitive regard for others, resulting in a complete dismissal of his own needs, which led the young boy to consider taking his own life.

❤

Unjust Punishment

Stripped down to his underwear, five-year-old Chris hears the snap of his father's belt as he and his sister, Katniss, stand side by side in their parents' bedroom. His father, Roland, comes from behind and circles the children, belt in hand, cautioning them not to move—it will only make it worse. Roland raises his arm, and Chris focuses on the silver belt buckle glimmering in the glow of the overhead light, then closes his eyes and retreats into the darkness.

When Chris wakes the next morning, a sharp pain shoots up his back. He raises his pajama top and counts the number of raised welts. Eight in all. Then he checks his legs and finds even more, each in varying shades of purple and brown. Grabbing the cover off his bed, the young boy wraps it around him and burrows inside it, his private cocoon. Then he climbs back into bed. There will be no Kindergarten for him—not until the marks have healed.

The smile, which lit up his face and his light blue eyes when he entered the café, quickly fades after recounting the all too vivid memory.

"[There were] leather belt marks from the middle of my back to the middle of my knees," Chris says.

Although his mother, Sylvie, never engaged in the beatings, she did nothing to stop it and was thus a conspirator. Chris is quick to acquit her of wrongdoing, a common occurrence of abused children, according to the experts.

"She wasn't abusive. She just didn't do anything about it," Chris says.

Unfortunately, the extreme level of maltreatment Chris experienced is a reality for a larger percentage of children of divorce than one would expect. An expert in the field of child welfare and principal investigator on the University of Michigan site of National Child Welfare Workforce Institute, Kathleen Coulborn Faller, offers evidence to this fact. She cites the study by the California Family Court, which reported 80 percent of divorced families experience problems including one or more of the following: child sexual abuse, child physical abuse, child neglect, substance abuse, domestic violence, and criminal activity.

The Pain of Abandonment

In addition to the extreme level of dysfunctionality exhibited by his parents, Chris and his sister fell victim to a different form of abuse—abandonment. Months before Chris's parents divorced, Roland left the family home, leaving his children in the care of their mother. Once the divorce was finalized, Sylvie made a move of her own.

Chris stood at the door and watched his mother pack the last of her boxes into her car.

"Where's your stuff, Chris? We have to get going," she said.

Chris reached behind him and held out a duffel bag. "It's all in here, Mom. Where is our new home?" he asked.

Sylvie shook her head, then signaled for Chris to get in the car. "You're going to your dad's place. My new apartment is an adults-only complex," she said taking her seat behind the wheel.

Chris reached out and grabbed his mother's hand. Looking down at her son's wrinkled nose and raised eyebrows, it was obvious to Sylvie that Chris was unfamiliar with the term adults-only. So she put it in plain terms for him.

"My place doesn't allow children," she said. "That means you and your sister can't live with me, so you'll be staying with your dad."

Chris's pale blue eyes widened, and his chin began to quiver.

"We don't get to live with you anymore?" Chris asked, blinking back his tears.

"It's getting late. We better go. Katniss will meet up with you at your dad's later," she said, ignoring her son's question.

Chris did as he was told and got in the passenger seat of his mother's Ford, tears streaming down the young boy's face.

"But don't you love us anymore?" Chris asked, his lip trembling.

Sylvie avoided her son's stare and busied herself with adjusting the rearview mirror. "Put your seat belt on." she said as she pulled away from the curb.

Chris's eyes once again fill with tears as he recalls the event that took place nearly 40 years ago.

"I remember feeling that it was not fair that I didn't get to have a mommy and a daddy like everybody else," Chris says. "It wasn't so much it hurt my feelings that she moved into the apartment complex, which it did, but the bigger thing was that it didn't seem to bother her. That was the thing that hurt more. I do remember that."

Disappointment Continues

Overnight stays weren't an option for Chris on his weekend visits with his mother. In an attempt to make up for this lack of time, she promised special outings with him and his sister. Unfortunately, many of those promises resulted in disappointment. Not long after she moved out, Chris woke early on a Saturday morning excited for his mother's visit. As he peered out his bedroom window, searching for her car, he called to his sister.

"Hurry up, Katniss," Chris said. "Mom's taking us to McDonald's for breakfast, and we need to be ready when she gets here."

Katniss emerged from the children's shared bathroom and plopped down on her brother's bed.

"She'll probably be late, Chris. She usually is," Katniss said. "Or it'll be like last time, so don't get too excited."

Chris shook his head, his dark blond hair badly in need of a trim.

"She'll show up this time. I know she will. Remember, Mom said she got sick last time. That's why she didn't come for us," Chris said, taking another quick peek out the window.

Like a sentry at his post, Chris remained stationed at the window for the next few hours. Nearing lunchtime, Katniss—who'd given up on her mother—returned to their room.

"She forgot us again, Chris. You might as well have lunch with me," she said as she joined him at the window.

"Maybe she'll come for us tomorrow," he said as he wiped the tears from his cheeks.

"Well, if she doesn't, little brother, you've always got me," Katniss said as she pulled him into a bear hug.

Recalling those early years, Chris is reminded of his sister's love and support.

"It was us against them," Chris says. "We just kind of held each other's hand—at least we had each other. We were really bonded by that."

Life With Dad

Life with Roland only perpetuated the cycle of abandonment for Chris. Not long after the divorce, Roland's parents passed away, which resulted in a large inheritance for their son. The newly acquired money gave Roland the freedom he'd always longed for.

"He spent all of it basically on drugs and hookers," Chris says. "And then he bought a house, which ended up being repossessed. He was doing a lot of drugs back then."

Countless times Chris recalls he and his sister were left to fend for themselves. Reflecting back on that time, it's obvious that for Chris, some wounds never heal.

"We were home alone all the time," Chris says. "Honestly, I feel lucky that my sister and I didn't burn the house down. Anything could have happened to us. Nobody would have known. I don't think anybody would have cared, really."

His parents' irresponsible actions led Chris to develop a sense of wariness of all people.

"I feel like I developed a hard candy shell," Chris says with a smile, proof of his indelible sense of humor. "I never trusted either one of them again, really. It makes me super mistrustful of people, and it makes me wait for the other shoe to drop, constantly."

Unexpected Changes

Adjusting to his mother's absence was difficult enough for Chris, but a few years later, after Sylvie moved to a new place that allowed children, Katniss joined her. His sister's move came as quite a shock and disappointment to Chris.

"It was probably four or five years that my sister and I lived apart," Chris says.

Although Chris hated being separated from his sister, he remained at his father's, not wanting him to be alone. Unbeknownst to Chris, Roland had orchestrated his daughter's move, as he no longer wanted her living with him.

"I figured it would be fair if each parent had one kid, and then nobody's feelings would get hurt," Chris says. "I wanted them both to feel loved and to know that they didn't do anything wrong, and that I wasn't mad at them."

Chris's heightened sense of sensitivity for others was a direct byproduct of his parents' divorce, and over the years it escalated to an alarming degree.

"I was so emotional that I would choose the clothes I would wear to school based on the last time I wore something because I didn't want to hurt the shirt's feelings by not wearing it often enough," Chris says.

"Children's Perspectives on Divorce," a study conducted in 2000 by the Australian Institute of Family Studies, consisting of interviews with fifteen children of divorce indicates how children see themselves as playing a key role in shaping social interactions and feel considerable responsibility for the wellbeing of their loved ones. These findings may explain Chris's oversensitivity. The study also points out that a child's interpretation of their world helps shape the coping strategies they adopt later in life.

"Like adults, children's needs and competencies vary," the study states. "We need to help children to define their situations in appropriate ways and to understand the limits of their responsibilities."

Much Needed Help

As much as Chris needed professional counseling, which could have addressed his need to adopt healthier coping strategies, that resource was made available to him only once by his parents.

"[Mom] was on this AA kick about talking, and she got me, well the insurance company got me, a therapist to talk to," Chris says. "I would talk to him every two weeks, mostly about the relationship I had with my parents. The big thing was just to spend more time with me. So, she would take me to the movies, or we would go play putt-putt golf. That lasted about three months. I don't know if the insurance stopped paying for the therapy, or if my mom was tired of driving me there. So that was the only time it was brought up, and it did help. I felt like I had an ally. Even though I only saw him for three months, I still remember his name."

Experts agree that counseling can prove beneficial for children of divorce, but it does depend on the child. They also stress a parent should never force a child into therapy.

Shannon sees benefits for both child and parent. "Oftentimes, co-parenting can be really helpful to work for the best interest for the child when there's a conflict," she says. "So, I think to have a place, to have a sounding board with someone who is familiar with the divorce process and can sometimes guide you and say, 'I don't recommend that, and this is why [can be helpful]."

With no other means of support after his counseling ended, Chris began questioning the meaning of family.

"It's not just the loss of the family unit; it's the loss of the definition of what a family is," Chris says. "Once those people decide to get a divorce, and your whole world goes upside down, you no longer know what family means. Relationship, love, marriage—you don't know what any of those words mean anymore.

"When you're a little kid, the only—or the closest—representation that you have to love, or a relationship, is that family. If that breaks up, then you don't know what love means anymore. So, then your definition of love is shattered, and you have to rebuild it, and you have to look somewhere to find it, and some people never do."

Considering the extent of his neglect and abuse, it's not surprising Chris succumbed to bouts of depression. During a weekend visit with his mother and sister, his depressive state escalated to a harmful degree. Although Chris's recollections differ from his sister's (as were depicted in the previous chapter), one thing is clear—both children held little hope for their future.

Sylvie brushed past her son who was trailing behind her, like a lost puppy, as she readied herself for a night out.

"Why can't you stay home with us, Mom?" he pleaded. "I'll be a good boy."

Ignoring his pleas, Sylvie headed for the door. "I'm sure there's something to eat for dinner," she said, adding, "Don't wait up."

As she closed the door behind her, Katniss grabbed her brother's hand and led him into the kitchen. After a thorough search of the refrigerator, where all she found was a rotten apple, a carton of expired milk, and half a loaf of stale bread, Katniss grimaced and moved on to the cabinets. A moment later, she called out.

"Look, Chris, I found Ramen noodles," she said. "Dinner in just a few minutes, little brother. At least noodles fill you up."

Chris took a seat at the kitchen table while his sister heated water on the stove. At nine years old, he'd become adept at keeping his emotions intact, but around his sister, he found it impossible to keep them hidden. Chris's vision clouded as he watched her prepare their dinner.

"Why does Mom keep doing this to us?" he asked, his voice shaky and broken.

The teakettle whistled, and Katniss filled two mugs with hot water and noodles, handing one to Chris. "You need to eat," she said.

Chris lowered his head into his hands and mumbled. "I'm not hungry." Katniss slammed her hand on the table, and her eyes grew wide. "You always do this," she yelled. "Why do you let them get you so upset? They're not worth it." Chris reached out and took his sister's hand. "I'm sorry. It's just Mom and Dad are supposed to take care of us," he said. Then with his voice rising in pitch, he added. "It's not fair."

Chris released his sister's hand, stood up, and ran to the bathroom. A moment later, he returned with a bottle of aspirin. He shook out a large handful of white tablets, tossed them in his mouth, then washed them down with the noodles. Katniss reached for the bottle and did the same. "I'm not staying here without you, little brother," she said.

Staring at the empty bottle, Katniss took her brother by the hand and led him down the hallway. When they arrived at their room, the children embraced each other with tears in their eyes before crawling into their beds.

"We fell asleep fully expecting not to wake up," Chris says. "I have no idea why we lived. To be honest, I cried when I woke up because that meant that God didn't want me either."

Chris takes a long sip of his coffee before explaining the choice he and his sister made that day.

"If this is what our lives had been so far, when the people we knew best were in charge of it, how were we going to make it any better?" he says, shaking his head. "Why stick around? If that's what an adult is like, I don't want to be an adult."

Escape From Reality

After the failed suicide attempt, Chris was in desperate need of some form of escapism, so he turned to his books.

"I kind of got lost in other realities," Chris says. "They weren't self-help books, and they weren't encyclopedias; they were stories. Initially, that was my escape—all of these books. I'm a sucker for a romantic comedy. I love fairy tales and romance, actual romance where people do things for each other because they want to, not to try and get something from it. And so I think I redefined my definition of love from all this 'chick shit.' I think that gave me a good base."

Life Choices

During his freshman year of high school, Chris was confronted with yet another change when his father divorced his second wife, Eileen, and moved in with his girlfriend.

"When my dad moved out, much like when my mom moved out, there was no room for me. He moved in with his girlfriend in a trailer," Chris said.

Fortunately, Eileen allowed Chris to stay with her after Roland left, and over the next two years, Chris tried to move forward with his life, but by his junior year, he feared the choices he'd made had led him down the same path as his father's.

"I dropped out [of school], got a job, got married, and had a baby a little while later," Chris says. "[My wife and I] rented a trailer. It was actually a single-wide trailer divided into two, so I guess technically it was half of a trailer. But hey, it was ours," Chris says.

Not long after their son Frank, was born, Chris and his wife separated. "At the time of the separation, my son lived with his mother, and she was pregnant with what we both thought could not possibly be my child," Chris explains. "This was the main reason for our marriage failing."

The separation prompted Chris to move back to Eileen's, but after an invitation from his friend to rent a room in his home, Chris moved out. Six months later, Chris was notified by the authorities that his wife had attempted suicide.

"They called me because on paper we were still married," Chris says.

"I decided right there, during that phone call, that she was not stable enough for my son to live with her. [Frank] lived with me from that day until he moved out to go to culinary school after he graduated high school."

Frank's mother was allowed visitations with her son, although countless times she was a no-show. "She was not dependable and never really had a relationship with Frank until after he was an adult, and [he decided to] reconnect with her on his own terms."

Fortunately for Frank, his relationship with Eileen has never faltered, and she continues to play a major role in his life.

"My son just calls Eileen 'Grandma.' That's Grandma to him," Chris says. "I still see her fairly regularly—more regularly than I see my dad. She's amazing."

A few years later, Chris gave marriage a second chance, but unfortunately, it also ended in divorce. He readily admits that in both instances, he had no concept of what made up a successful marriage.

"In my life, there wasn't a lot of effort put in any relationship I saw," Chris says. "So, I think that affected how I chose my first two wives and how I treated them and how we treated each other. Your experiences inform your selection, and I don't think that I selected the right people. And because I didn't select the right people, they didn't treat me the way I should have been treated, and I didn't treat them the way they should have been treated."

According to Scott, adult children of divorce often try to heal childhood hurts through personal relationships.

"We want somebody else to heal that wound," Scott says. "It is really common for human beings to connect with somebody, to reach out and try and fill that void with someone else, and what ends up happening is that person has a missing piece, and so that's why we're drawn together. If we don't work through that stuff [on our own], it doesn't end up working because we're following the same pattern. The only one who can heal that [past hurt] is the person themselves."

Over the years, when Chris was faced with parental decisions, he'd consider how his father would handle it—and then do the exact opposite.

"I use my parents as a role model because they taught me what *not* to do," Chris says. Chris is happy to report that Frank, now in his late twenties, is single, living on his own, and doing great. "And Frank doesn't have any kids. He says I made it look so hard, so why would he do that anytime soon," Chris adds with a smile.

As a twice-divorced father, Chris is well aware of the obstacles faced by parents during a divorce. He speaks from experience and cautions parents not to let their own emotions get in the way of prioritizing their child's welfare during this difficult time.

"I know that there are a lot of moving parts, and your brain is really not focused where it would normally be. You're focused on all this other stuff," Chris says. "I think the kid can get lost in that; the actual caring for the kid can get lost in all that. I would just say take care of your kid. Don't forget to take care of your kid."

Although Sylvie's relationship with her son never improved, she devoted the last twenty years of her life to helping emotionally and mentally challenged children and teens. After her passing, the institution she worked with founded an award in her honor.

"I feel it was her way to atone for how she treated her own children," Chris says.

In past years Chris has presented the award named after his mother, and each time it has been a reminder of the drastic difference between the mother he knew and the woman who provided help to so many troubled children.

Before budgetary restrictions put an end to the annual ceremony, Katniss had the honor of presenting the award. "She was moved to tears hearing these people speak glowingly about our mom," Chris says. "And all of these people that talk about all these wonderful things my mom did, is kind of diametrically opposed to the mother I knew."

Over the years, Chris made numerous attempts to discuss with Sylvie how her behavior affected him. Each time he was met with claims of either denial or a feigned inability to recall any such instances. Still, there is one aspect of his life in which he gives her full credit.

"The greatest thing that my mother ever did, which had the greatest impact on my life, was she introduced me to my current wife," Chris says.

He credits his past relationship failures for the success of his current marriage. Considering he and his wife are coming up on their twentieth anniversary, his reasoning justified.

"I try the hardest to be a good partner and a good friend and a good person to my wife," Chris says. "All of her friends cannot believe our relationship."

Regarding his relationship with his father, Chris describes it as guarded.

"I am a better person than he was, or is, and so is my son. I turned out this good despite of him—not because of him," Chris says. "I just respond to him when I want to, and I don't when I don't want to."

Over the years, Chris developed a unique perspective on life and love, one that has served him well.

"Here's the way I look at it. My parents had this little sculpture that I called love, and then my parents got a divorce, and they smashed it to pieces," Chris says. "Then I didn't have any more sculpture. From all these books and all these stories, I managed to cobble together a pretty decent sized amount of clay, and then, over the years, I sculpted that piece of clay little by little into what I think love is now."

My Thoughts

Just like Chris, my son experienced abuse at the hands of his father, and I allowed it to happen. I can never make up for that. During my marriage, my fear overruled my instinct to protect my son, resulting in over ten years of physical and emotional abuse for us both.

As determined as I was about removing us from that toxic environment, I found I was still plagued with an all-consuming fear. What if I failed to provide my son the life he deserved? What if we couldn't make it on our own? So, in the midst of this confusing and transforming time, what I should have offered my son was honesty about how uncertain I felt, but instead of owning up to my many worries and fears, I lied to him and reassured him time and again that we would be fine.

This was yet another of my mistakes. Because as I was experiencing confusion, anger, and fear as we traveled this unknown territory. So was my son. If I had shared my true feelings with him instead of trying to put on a brave front, he would have benefited from the understanding that he was not alone in how he felt.

During this difficult time of transition, as much as our children need our love and support, they also need our honesty, even when we make mistakes—especially when we make mistakes. I believe it's how we handle those failures that teach our children a valuable life lesson. All people make mistakes, even parents. By our admission of this fact, we reassure our children that as parents we understand

and accept that they too will make mistakes. And when they do, we will continue to love them unconditionally, as we hope they will love us. Moving forward in this journey of uncertainty with understanding and honesty offers your child the gift of assurance that you are still a family, maybe not the same as before, but a family all the same. ❤

CHAPTER NINE

ANDY

Two months after his tenth birthday, Andy's parents announced their separation. Six months later, the couple divorced, and the young boy's life was indelibly changed. As an only child, Andy looked to his parents for reassurance during this difficult time of transition. Unfortunately, his father chose to distance himself from his son, and his mother, feeling as confused and unsure of their future as Andy, enlisted the help of professionals rather than offer her son the support he needed. As it turned out, what Andy needed most was time to adjust and accept the confusing family dynamics taking place in his life.

Breaking the News

Standing in the doorway to her son's room, Andy's mom, Kayla, called to him as he played with his Hot Wheels.

"Dad and I want to talk to you. Let's go in the living room, okay?"

Andy raised his head, pushing his glasses up against his nose. "Can we talk later?" the ten-year-old asked, his attention turning back to his cars.

His mother's eyes filled with tears, and her voice began to quiver. "No, honey, we need to talk now." She signaled for him to follow.

When they reached the living room, the boy noticed immediately something was different. Andy's father, Greg, was seated on the couch with his back straight and his face drawn, and the TV was off. It was never off when his father was home. Andy felt his stomach tighten when his mother patted the sofa, signaling him to join them.

"Your dad and I are going to separate for a little while," she said in a rush. "All that means right now is your dad is moving—to the basement."

Greg added. "I'll still be here."

Kayla looked from her husband to her son. "This is not an official divorce," she said. "But yeah, Dad's moving downstairs."

Staring wide-eyed at them both, Andy asked, "Then what?"

Greg glared at his wife like she was the dealer holding all the cards.

"Then we go from there, but we have to do this to get to there," she said.

Andy, now forty-one, a successful artist, accomplished writer, and photographer, sits back in his chair and releases an audible sigh.

"My mom and dad breaking the news in front of me, leaning in like we were all in a huddle, was the first and only time I felt like an equal," Andy says. "Like being invited up from the kids' table. It felt like graduation."

Although his initial reaction was one of solidarity, like most children of divorce living in a dysfunctional environment, Andy assumed his family was like everyone else's, and was blindsided by his parents' announcement.

"Because even bad can be normal," Andy explains. "My family's normal is my only basis of comparison, my only frame of reference for families. So if my home is normal, then a normal home sounds like fighting."

Collom confirms Andy's line of rationalization, explaining that any child growing up in a dysfunctional family accepts that environment as normal.

"If [parents] argue a lot, if there's a lot of volatility, that's just normal to them," Collom says. "But to break that up, it's devastating."

He stresses parents use an age-appropriate manner when presenting this type of news to a child.

"Sitting down and talking about [the divorce] doesn't work for children until they develop emotionally," he says. "They get it through how we attend to them. They get it through how we play with them, and they get it through how we interact with them and attentiveness more than anything."

Separation vs. Divorce

The only move Greg made during the separation was downstairs to the remodeled basement. With his parents living separate lives—albeit while still residing in the same home—Andy was offered a glimpse into what life might look like if his parents divorced.

"After the separation, when Mom's not crying, Dad's not yelling, and you're playing quietly, it's hard to argue with calm results," Andy says with a smile.

The couple separated in March, and two months later, Kayla filed for divorce, prompting Greg to finally move out.

"Dad oddly moved a few blocks away," Andy says. "So there was very little adjusting. I could walk or bike to Dad's without breaking a sweat. Hell, in the early days, I'd walk Chi-Chi, the family dog, from Mom's house to Dad's, and back again. It was kind of nice until Chi-Chi passed."

The proximity of his parents' homes made the physical separation an easy transition, but the difficulty for Andy came in adjusting to two very different environments.

"Ten-year-old me lived between two planets—planet Dad and planet Mom," Andy says. "Planet Dad was dark, cold, and fast food scented. Planet Mom was warm, inviting, and home-cooked. Growing up, my dad was reserved, and I held out hope that if I hung around him that maybe he'd warm up to me, but no. To Dad—I can only assess—I was little more than a reminder of Mom, and Dad didn't want to remember Mom. Dad's weekends became my first exposure to speed dating."

The custody agreement provided Andy with biweekly weekend visitation with his father, while residing the remainder of the time with his mother. This came about due to Kayla's determination to do only what was best for Andy, which included retaining ownership of the family home in order to secure one constant for her son during this time of uncertainty.

"Mom fought for full custody immediately and aggressively, and I thank her for it," Andy says.

Age Matters

Experts agree every child feels the impact of their parents' divorce, and according to Collom, many times, the child's personality plays a determining factor as to the significance of that impact.

"Some are better at it than others. I would call it ego strength related," Collom says. "The child who has better ego strength is able to deal with crises, feel good about themselves. They're able to deal with tragedy and crises in general."

Andy doesn't deny the effect his parents' divorce had on him, but he believes he was at an age that allowed him to accept it and move on.

"If I were younger, I doubt I'd have registered the change in tone after the divorce," Andy says. "And if I were older, I definitely would've acted out more."

Admittedly, age is a determining factor in how children handle divorce. According to Minerva, there is a greater potential for disruption for children fourteen years of age and younger.

Scott agrees. "I would say it's definitely more detrimental for younger children simply because they don't have the skills to process or talk about it, and it becomes so much more internalized and [they believe], it's their fault because that's how their development works."

As for parents who shy away from divorce, believing it's better for their children, Scott cautions, they should think again.

"When parents stay in unhealthy relationships they don't show their children the remodeling, they don't show their children their own healing, they don't show their children we can make mistakes, and we can heal from them," Scott says.

Stuck in the Middle

Even if it's an unconscious decision, parental alienation is a common occurrence with divorced parents. Andy experienced this type of behavior on his biweekly weekend visits when he found himself an unwitting partner in his father's spy games.

Loading up his backpack in preparation for his weekend with his dad, Andy called out to his mom, "What time is it?"

Kayla checked the clock, then headed to her son's room. "It's almost 7:00 p.m.," she said.

Andy looked up when she entered his room, then grabbed his backpack. "We've got to get going. Dad said he'd take me to get snow cones."

Minutes later, they were in the car on their way to Greg's house. Upon arrival, Andy jumped out of the car, gave his mother an obligatory wave, and then climbed the front porch steps. When his father met him at the door, Andy offered up a big smile. Opening the door, Greg ignored his son and kept his focus on his ex-wife's car as it made its way down the street.

"Where'd Mom say she was going tonight?" he asked.

Andy dropped his backpack on the floor, then looked up at his dad. "She's going to her mom's."

Greg shut and locked the front door then signaled for Andy to follow him out to the garage. "Come on," he called, "We're going for a drive."

Andy smiled wide in anticipation of his trip to the snow cone stand. "Okay," he said, as he ran after him.

Half an hour later, Andy found himself still in the car as his dad cruised the same street over and over. In fact, they were moving so slowly Andy thought they might as well get out and walk. After what seemed like the hundredth pass, Greg turned to his son and asked. "Where was mom going?"

"Grandma's house," Andy said.

Greg pointed to the parked cars lined up and down the street where his ex-mother-in-law lived. "You see Mom's car anywhere?" he asked his son.

Andy shook his head no and then watched his father's smile morph into a sneer as he gunned the engine and then tore off down the street.

"Wonder where she really is?" he asked when they reached the end of the block, adding, "It's time to go home."

Andy's nose wrinkled as he stared at his dad. "I thought we were getting snow cones." he said.

Greg shook his head and avoided his son's gaze. "Snow cones aren't open," he answered.

Turning away from his father, Andy stared out the window and then slid back into his seat. There wouldn't be any special treats this weekend.

Andy was also subjected to repeated interrogations by his father on his biweekly visits.

"Dad wants to know how Mom spent his child support check," Andy says. "Dad wants to drive by Grandma's again. Dad's depressed, and obsessed, and I'm riding shotgun with nowhere good to go. I don't blame Mom for this. Dad still doesn't yell or hit like before—for that alone it's worth another no headlights drive by."

According to Terranova, experts view this type of parental alienation as a form of child abuse.

"When a child is being split out from one parent to the other and being drawn into emotional situations that really have nothing to do with that child's developmental needs, the more a parent puts a child in the middle, the worse the outcome, in my opinion," she says.

Terranova suggests parents should speak up for each other for the child's sake.

"The child needs to know there is still some level of united front, if at all possible," she says. "That level of healthy restraint is good for a child to see."

She suggests using phrases like, "You know your dad has a lot of hurt feelings," or, "He's having a hard time knowing how to do all of this, and he's mad at me," as a way of explaining a parent's negative actions to the child.

Scott agrees that parents offering children examples of respectful behavior with one another is beneficial for them to witness.

"It is absolutely devastating to see a parent badmouthing the other parent and not realize how detrimental that is to the child," she says, adding parents must separate their role of husband or wife from that of the parent.

"[The children] are not meant to be in the intimate details of the husband and wife relationship." Scott says. "The biggest thing you can do is to say [to the child] over and over and over, 'This is between the two of us, and whatever is happening to us has nothing to do with you.'"

According to Minerva, a parent inquiring what took place at the other parent's home, "makes the child feel like they are in the middle of something," she says, "Children can also learn to manipulate their parents, so the more open communication between the parents, the better for the children."

Seeking Help

While Andy was subjected to his father's interrogations and erratic behavior, life with his mother included its own set of frustrations. Kayla felt incapable of providing the guidance and support her son needed while dealing with her fears and doubts after the divorce. Despite her son's verbal opposition to the idea of therapy, which he voiced often, Kayla insisted Andy attend group counseling at his school, in addition to evening sessions at the counseling center she frequented.

"As a kid, you don't add to the initial divorce conversation—it's happening. You're just brought up to speed," Andy says. "I would've liked to experience the divorce before counselors fed me their guesses as to what I'm about to experience. Both group settings were with kids older and younger than me. Our unity came from divorce.

"Inexperienced nuns and counselors parroted work sheets and lesson plans addressing generalities. You're led to believe anything you say doesn't leave the room—but it does. You're a minor, and your parents will be told. I was not open in my sessions, and on the last day of one of the groups, I merely hid under a table until I saw my mom's feet at the door," Andy says. He recommends parents give the child time to comprehend this new definition of family before considering counseling.

"Let them experience this so-called divorce thing before assuming that anyone but you, the parent, can help them," Andy says. "In short, I felt rushed and generalized, which resulted in me being an unwilling participant. When you lump kids of all ages together, you feel corralled, labeled, and annoyed.

"This whole divorce ball started rolling with my mom and dad assuring me nothing, to very little, would change, yet I found myself grouped among the outcasts, other kids of divorce, talking about how weird we all felt. Divorce is forever; most kids can't contemplate forever. Give the effects of divorce time to take effect. As a kid, I wish future me had asked for a conversation about divorce rather than being given a presentation."

Andy's home environment before the divorce certainly didn't promote self-expression. According to Minerva, for a child lacking open communication within the family unit, the idea of counseling may not be the best choice.

"To take [a child] to some stranger and say, 'Now talk. Tell them how you feel,' could lead to resistance," she says.

Each child is different, so work with your child to determine the best way to provide the support and guidance they need during this time of transition. For those children open to the idea of counseling, Collom suggests parents look for kid-friendly environments in the therapist's office and meeting with the therapist in advance.

Testing His Limits

The mantra "children of divorce tend to act out" was repeated time and again by Andy's counselors and parents. A year after the divorce, he decided to test this theory.

Leaving work late Friday afternoon, Kayla was eager to begin her vacation. She decided to stop at home before picking Andy up at the neighbor's. Then they'd head out for burgers and fries to celebrate. As she slid her key in the front door, she heard the phone, so she rushed inside, grabbed the receiver off the wall, only to discover an unfamiliar voice on the other end.

"Is this Kayla Scott?" a man asked.

"Yes, who is this?" she said, setting her keys down on the kitchen table.

He cleared his throat before introducing himself. "This is Kenneth Bradshaw, with Venture Security. I have your son in custody, Mrs. Scott. He was caught shoplifting," he said.

Kayla grabbed the back of the chair and swallowed hard. "Is he alright?" she asked.

The man lowered his voice and whispered into the phone. "Other than being scared out of his wits, I'd say he's fine," he said with a slight chuckle, then added, "We need you to come pick him up."

Nodding, it took Kayla a moment to realize she needed to answer verbally. "Of course. I'll be right over," she said.

Hanging up the phone, Kayla felt the sudden sensation of déjà vu. Several years ago, she received a similar phone call from the security department at Target. Greg had been caught shop lifting, and he had taken Andy with him. The nightmare that followed the incident is one she'd hoped never to experience again. Now her son was in trouble, and he needed her. Attempting to clear the painful memory from her thoughts, Kayla shook her head and then grabbed her keys and rushed out the door.

Time seemed endless to Andy as he sat with his wrists handcuffed behind him on a metal chair in the cramped security room, all the while maintaining a constant vigil on the office door. Directly across from him sat two of his neighborhood friends, accomplices in the theft, also in handcuffs and with their heads bowed.

When the door finally opened, and his mother walked in, their eyes locked. Although he fought his instinct to cry, once he saw the tears streaming down her cheeks, that battle was lost. Then Mr. Bradshaw approached Kayla and offered his hand.

"Thanks for coming so quickly," he said.

"What happens now?" Kayla asked.

Bradshaw leaned in and whispered, "The store's not going to press charges," he said. "I think this scare has been enough."

Turning away from Kayla, Bradshaw approached Andy.

"Young man, I hope you learned a lesson today. Now that your mom's here, you are free to go," he said, unlocking the cuffs.

The young boy walked silently behind his mother, rubbing his wrists as they made their way out of the store. Each remained silent on the car ride home. Once they arrived, Kayla sent Andy to his room, and she joined him a few minutes later.

"I can't tell you how upset I am," she said, her voice quivering and tears streaming down her face. "I can't trust myself to talk to you right now, so I want you to stay in your room. I'm going to take a drive, try and sort things out in my head. When I get back, we'll talk. Do you understand me?"

Andy silently nodded, then watched his mother turn away from him. When the front door slammed shut, he ran to the basement, gathered up his cache, and stuffed it into a bag. He brought the bag upstairs and hid it under his bed. Then he sat and waited.

Moments after hearing the key in the front door, his mother appeared in the doorway to his room. With the glow of the kitchen light behind her, Andy noticed her eyes were still red as she walked toward him.

"Okay, time to talk," she said, swallowing hard as though trying to force down a pill. "Just answer me one question. Why?"

Andy's eyes filled with tears. "The other kids said it would be fun," he said. Then he added in a whisper, "And I'd seen Dad do it."

Kayla's eyes widened, and her hand flew to her mouth.

"You remember that? Since you never talked about that night, I thought—well I'd hoped—you'd forgotten. Your dad should never have done that, and he should never have taken you with him," she said, shaking her head.

"I'm so sorry you had to be a part of that, and I'm sorry I never talked to you about it," she added.

Andy shook his head, and then lowered his eyes. "Yeah, I remember."

Forcing herself to keep calm, Kayla explained, "But what you did tonight is just as wrong. Do you understand? And the worst part of all is that now I feel like I can't trust you," she said, her voice catching in her throat. "I've *always* trusted you, Andy."

"I promise, Mom, I won't do it again," he said. Then he jumped up, reached under his bed, and pulled out the hidden bag.

"Look, here's all the other stuff I stole, but I won't steal again, Mom," Andy said, dumping the contents of the bag—batteries, Hot Wheels, pens, pencils, gum, candy, all of it onto his bed.

Kayla scanned the collection and then pointed at a brightly wrapped package.

"Why did you steal those?" she said, referring to a package of condoms laying in the middle of his stash.

Andy just shook his head. "I don't know. I don't even know what they're for," he said.

Kayla laughed out loud, finding she could suddenly breathe. Then she reached out and pulled Andy to her.

"I'll explain those later. What I want you to know now is how proud I am that you showed me this," she said. "Thank you. But there's one more thing you need to do. You have to call your father."

Minutes later, Andy held the kitchen phone in his hand, listening to it ring on the other end. When Greg answered, Kayla, who listened from the extension in her bedroom, spoke first.

"Your son has something he needs to tell you," she said.

A few moments of silence followed before Andy spoke.

"Dad, I got caught shoplifting at Venture tonight. Mom had to come and get me," he said in a low whisper.

Andy held his breath as he waited for a response.

"Did you hear what your son said?" Kayla asked.

"Yes, I heard," Greg finally answered. "Why did you do that?"

Without a moment's hesitation, Andy's voice rising in volume answered, "Because I saw *you* do it, Dad."

Once again, there was silence. Kayla hung up the extension, walked to the kitchen, grabbed the phone from her son's hand, and slammed it down. Then she opened her arms wide, and Andy gratefully accepted her embrace.

"Never forget, no matter what, I will always love you," Kayla said.

Andy shook his head and squeezed her as tight as he could.

Recalling the incident, the memory evokes a deep sadness in Andy's blue eyes.

"When Mom's wet, red eyes finally caught mine, I couldn't lift my head again for hours," he says. "The shame and pain I caused her was not a high to chase but a low to avoid—pure shame."

The Disadvantage of Being an Only Child

According to the experts, an only child takes their parents' divorce quite personal in comparison to children with siblings.

"All children think it's their fault. It's just the only child is more adultized and aware of all the things that are going on around them, so there's nobody to bounce it off of and make sense of it all," Collom says.

Luckily for Andy, he found an ally in his own home. One morning as he sorted Legos on the kitchen table, he sought refuge from that trusted friend when his father's loud and livid voice resonated through the house. Dropping the plastic pieces onto the table, Andy made his way to the basement stairs. Before heading down, he peeked in the living room and saw his mother seated on the couch, her head in her hands. His father paced in front of her, waving his arms in the air, his face turning a deep shade of crimson.

Andy hurried down the stairs, slid open the door, and then silently shut it behind him. Standing in the darkness of the basement, he called out in a whisper, "Chi-Chi. Here, girl."

A moment later, the collie made her way to the young boy, mimicking his silence. The only sound she made was the soft clicking of her nails on the concrete floor. Andy sat down, grabbed her, and pulled her to him, whispering, "Good girl," with a catch in his throat.

Chi-Chi emitted a small cry, and Andy wrapped his arms around her neck and then buried his tear-stained face in her fur. The two allies remained in their hidden shelter until the bellowing ceased upstairs.

"I hid in the basement and cried on the dog so as to not disturb the Kleenex stock," Andy says.

Someone New

With many divorced parents, the eventuality of introducing a new love interest into the family dynamic is inevitable. In these situations, according to Terranova, the child's willingness to accept this individual is often determined by the level of trust they have in the parent.

"Of course there are the variables of how a person is introduced, how quickly and how much of an opportunity the child's had to get to know this person before they're involved in parenting or trying to help out in the home," Terranova says.

Andy's acceptance of John, Kayla's friend from work, validates Terranova's theory.

"Looking back, I'm surprised I wasn't skeptical of John given our recent foul experience with Dad, but I wasn't, mainly because of Mom," Andy says. "With John came instant trust, his demeanor, and the fact he has Mom's stamp of approval. When Mom's excited to show off something good in her life, there's always a lot to love about that something good. John actually asked us what we'd like to do rather than tell us what we're in for."

John soon became a regular part of the family, spending evenings and weekends with Kayla and Andy. Their first Valentine's Day together, the trio went to the movies to see *Teenage Mutant Ninja Turtles*. Once John became a constant in their lives, Andy noticed a significant change in his mother's personality.

"Mom smiled with John. He smiled with her. They laughed together," Andy says. "The proof is in the pudding. They're good. They're happy. Mom and Dad weren't happy. Mom couldn't be happy for both her and Dad. With John, Mom has a partner."

Kayla and John's relationship was heading into its second year when she was invited to an out-of -town event. Volunteering to look after Andy while she was away, John's actions that weekend resulted in a bonding experience for Andy.

"I wasn't sure how things would go. I was better in small doses since I was just beginning my angsty teen years," Andy recalls. "In those days, all my exhales were heavy sighs, and I was maximum crabby. I feared for John's safety. To his credit, John stayed cool. If he was ever nervous, he never showed it, and unlike Dad, he asked three times a day if I was hungry.

"We'd watch bike tapes throughout the day, play video games, stop everything to watch the latest episode of *The Simpsons*, then movies at night. Over dinner, I'd try to stump him with Hollywood trivia. John was never stumped. He was unlike Dad in every positive way possible. He was the bad dad antidote."

Terranova explains that a child's personality plays a significant part in their adjustment to the new family member.

"Some children are very extroverted and kind of gravitate toward social relationships and interactions and may be more inclined," Terranova says. "While others may warm up very slowly and be more methodical and thoughtful and more introverted, and that child may need more time to bring someone new into their life. Certainly, it would be a good idea for a child to have an adjustment period before someone is invited into the family circle."

In Andy's case, his connection with John was immediate.

"John's likable in no time, [then you] add Mom's approval, and he's in line for sainthood," Andy says with a grin. "John watched *Ninja Turtles* with me and helped me put together a new *Turtles* sewer action playset. He played videogames with me. Bottom line: John's cool. John's so cool you hope to pick up any of his excess coolness. I attached myself immediately to him."

Moving Away and Moving On

Only a few months after Andy's high school graduation, John was offered a job in California, so the family, including Andy's high school girlfriend, Marley, drove across the country and settled into their West Coast home.

A few years after the move, the relationship between Andy and his father drew to a close, with Andy's one-way phone calls to Greg the only proof it had existed at all. Andy had come to the conclusion that as far as his dad was concerned, he was simply a reminder of past mistakes.

"The divorce is a loss. I remind you of that loss, and your pride will never heal," Andy says. "I didn't deserve your ire or your heavy hand. You'd sooner pop my zits than hug me. You bullied me for what I cost you, a life unlived and unknown."

As for his personal relationship, he and Marley have remained together for twenty-two years, and he's quick to admit not all of them have been easy.

"Our first two years together were mostly one extended fight," Andy says. "We wonder what kept us together. We wonder if we weren't just mimicking our models. This probably sounds like I'm blaming my mom and dad, but I'm thanking Mom and John for providing me proof that not all couples end, that true love prevails."

As solid as their relationship is today, Andy and Marley still resist taking the next step: marriage. Each credits being children of divorce as the reason.

"Not only am I a child of divorce, but I'm a Catholic child of divorce, so yeah, it's kind of made me want to avoid the whole thing until I'm 110 percent sure," Andy says, adding, "Weddings aren't a marriage so much as they're jewelry and paperwork. Marley and I have been together by choice for twenty-two years. That's a marriage."

Acceptance

Andy's acceptance that his parents are like everyone else—human beings who make mistakes—exemplifies his level of tolerance. His acceptance that life was better because of the divorce reveals his level of maturity.

"Things happen for a reason. Things also stop happening for a reason," Andy says. "Marriage is a chance you take together, a choice you make together, a change you make together. The wrong couple can get married at any age."

"As a kid, your parents' divorce is like the earth cracking in two. Picture yourself as a moon orbiting planet Mom-and-Dad, but that doomed planet ruptures at the core, then Mom-and-Dad split in half. As luck would have it, your moon still orbits Mom-and-Dad. The planets even stay close together after separating. Sometimes you circle planet Mom, then figure eight between them and orbit planet Dad.

As their kid, you're the last proof these two halves were one. What happens next is time—time to form a basis of comparison between planets. After the divorce, Mom hasn't stopped bettering herself to the world's benefit. After the divorce, Dad's bitter and distant or snarling. Divorce changed my dad in that he was left alone. Mom found her way out of Dad's rusty bear trap and still smiles, knowing she made the right move for her and me. She knows because I tell her."

My Thoughts

This chapter is extremely personal to me because this is my son's chapter. His honesty and humor convey our struggle as well as our perseverance during a time that was unlike any other. At the journey's end, we found our love and trust in one another had grown exponentially, despite the countless number of conflicts, disputes, and the whirlwind of emotions we both experienced.

Along that journey, my mistakes were many, and topping the list was my failure to offer my son what he needed most—a sense of belonging. The family he grew up with was no longer intact after the divorce, so where did that leave him? Instead of offering him answers to his questions, I focused on ensuring the bills were paid, that he had a roof over his head and food in his stomach. With my energies relegated to maintaining the necessities in life, I lost sight of his emotional needs, as many parents do during this time of transition.

Like a disease, which strips away the normalcy of life and replaces it with fear and anxiety, divorce, for a child, eradicates their instinct to trust, and leaves in its wake a consistent sense of uncertainty and alarm. By offering our children all we have to give—even if we feel it's not enough—we provide them a lifeline to cling to as they travel the uncharted path of uncertainty.

For both Andy and me, the memories of the past, good and bad, live with us. And despite those battle scars, our relationship has flourished beyond my greatest expectation. My wish is for this book to offer hope to those venturing down the same path my son and I traveled over thirty years ago. Hope that despite the mistakes and difficulties that lie ahead, one can emerge from these trials and tribulations all the stronger. My son and I are living proof that is possible.❤

CHAPTER TEN

MICHELLE

Michelle was ten months old at the time of her parents' divorce. The mature nature, an extramarital affair that led to the breakup, has never been fully disclosed to this smart and inquisitive ten-year-old. Michelle's frequent requests of the details behind their divorce made it obvious to both Kay and Ronnie, Michelle's parents, that the time to reveal to their only child just what took place over nine years before was fast approaching. The eventuality of this disclosure plagued them both.

*This chapter is a departure from the previous ones in that Kay, Michelle's mother, narrated it. The relationship between Kay and Ronnie offers a positive example of successful co-parenting, even in the most difficult situations.

♥

Unexpected Results

Ronnie walked through the front door of his home to find Kay, his wife, waiting for him in the entryway.

"I've scheduled an appointment with a marriage counselor for this Thursday," Kay said without taking a breath. "If you're not going to tell *me* why you've been acting weird, maybe you'll explain it to the therapist."

Ronnie remained silent as he walked to the kitchen with Kay trailing behind him. After her husband took a seat at the kitchen table, Kay steadied herself against the counter, anticipating a heated confrontation.

"Okay," Ronnie said, staring across the table at his wife. "We'll see the counselor."

Kay met his gaze, unable to hide her look of surprise at his easy acceptance. As she studied the face of the man she'd known since high school, a man she used to count on, who had never let her down, she wondered where that man had gone.

A year into their marriage, Ronnie was delighted when Kay told him she was pregnant. After Michelle was born, he appeared smitten with his infant daughter. But a few months later, his attitude toward her and Kay drastically changed.

The following Thursday, when the couple's session ended, they exited the therapist's office, Kay's eyes red and puffy. Ronnie followed behind her with a look of disinterest on his face. Their uncomfortable silence lasted the entire car ride home.

Ronnie pulled into the garage, paid the babysitter, and then went upstairs to the couple's bedroom. Kay moved through the house as if in a trance. On her way upstairs, she checked on Michelle, who was sound asleep in her crib. When she entered the master bedroom, she watched as Ronnie removed his clothes from the dresser drawers and then tossed them into a suitcase that lay open on the bed.

"What are you doing?" Kay said with a catch in her throat. "First, you don't say a word in therapy, and now this?"

Ronnie hovered over the half-filled suitcase, his hand full of socks.

"Kay, I don't love you, and I don't want to work on this," he said as he stared at the suitcase. "I just can't do this anymore. I'll be at my mom's if you need to get a hold of me."

Ronnie grabbed the suitcase and rushed past his wife on his way out of the room. A minute later, Kay heard the front door slam shut.

On an early spring afternoon, Kay recounts that momentous day, showing no sign of emotion as she methodically folds a stack of clean towels, still warm from the dryer. After setting them down, she leans back and releases a heavy sigh.

"It was probably two weeks tops when my world came crashing down," Kay says.

The Truth Comes Out

Soon after Ronnie's departure, the yearlong divorce proceedings began. Midway through the year, Kay accepted an invitation to meet with her husband.

Ronnie perched on the edge of the recliner as Kay studied him from her seat on the couch. As his eyes met hers, they shifted to his hands, which he held in his lap. Kay was surprised to see there were tears in his eyes.

"I know I haven't given you any explanation of why I left," Ronnie said as he stood up and started to pace the length of the room.

"The truth is, I've been having an affair," he said, keeping his focus on the floor.

Kay collapsed into the sofa, her body shaking uncontrollably.

"An affair," she said in a whisper. "With who?"

Ronnie shook his head.

"Tess. It started two years ago."

Kay sat up straight, walked over, and reached out and slapped her husband's face.

"Two years," she yelled. "That means the affair started right after we were married."

Kay's hand trembled as she lowered it from Ronnie's cheek and stared at its imprint still visible on his face.

"How could you do this to me? How could you do this to Michelle?"

"And she's pregnant," Ronnie said.

This sudden bombardment of deceit was almost too much for Kay. Not only had her husband lied and deceived her from the start of their marriage, but Tess, someone she considered her friend, was a conspirator in this deception as well.

Ronnie pleaded with Kay for her to take him back and help him raise his child. The fact that he thought she would accept this preposterous proposal was the crowning moment of clarity for Kay, and any previous thoughts of reconciliation were immediately dismissed from her mind.

Staying Connected

The divorce proceedings moved forward at this point, with Ronnie petitioning equal time with his daughter.

"He always wanted to be a part of her life. That was the hardest part," Kay says. "I think if anything, that made me more appreciative of the time I had with Michelle. In the very beginning, I felt like he wanted control, and he wanted to make sure that I didn't take her from him. He was definitely worried that he wouldn't get to see his child as much as he wanted to."

Custody battles are highly emotional times, and parents often lose sight of the child's welfare. But not so in Kay's situation.

"I gave her a lot of attention because I was worried about how she was doing and how the divorce would affect her. I felt like I needed to give her that extra attention because I was afraid of what these transitions were doing to her," Kay says.

Experts agree establishing one-on-one time with your child during times of transition can have positive results. Collom suggests that divorced parents go so far as to schedule dates with their children. Dedicating half an hour or so two or three times a week for one-on-one time with each child can help to counteract the disorienting effects of divorce. Collom suggests that parents "really focus on the child, doing what the child wants. Don't let outside activities come in." Minerva suggests what she calls *active listening*. "Have a conversation and not direct where it's going, but try to reflect what the child is saying in a way that helps them know that they've been understood."

A United Front

Throughout the divorce, Kay's first priority was always her daughter's welfare. Because of that, she succeeded in an area where many divorced parents fail—shielding Michelle from the negative feelings she had toward Ronnie.

Kay's approach is supported by Collom, who believes that presenting the child with a supportive front can be extremely beneficial, and he advises parents to set aside negative personal feelings so that their presentation to the child can be a united one.

"Hopefully, you have two healthy enough parents that can approach it in a way that's supportive toward the child. Stay neutral regarding how they feel about the spouse," Collom says.

Minerva cautions, "Keep any kind of conflict out of their direct observation. Kids will feel it anyway."

As for Kay, she advises parents to never let their children see the anger they feel for their ex-spouse. "It's only going to harm them,"

Kay says. "I think some parents think if I say negative things about the other parent they're going to want to be with them more. It really doesn't."

Age Matters

Kay believed Michelle was shielded from the trauma most children of divorce experience because she was only ten months old at the time it all began.

"She was such a colicky baby. I think for the first six months of her life, she cried every single night before bed, literally three hours straight. She just cried and cried," Kay recalls. "I didn't know what was affecting her."

According to Minerva, even a child not old enough to fully comprehend the concept or repercussions of divorce or separation may still be significantly impacted by their parents' decision.

"We know that in those first few years, zero to three, a sudden abandonment is really potentially devastating to the development of the child's psyche," Minerva says. "The fact that they don't have language means that it is recorded sensorily. They don't have the ability to reason. They just *feel* it. So, for a father to say, pick up his stuff and go, 'It's not going to really affect the kid long term,' oh, it affects them more than you know."

According to Collom, the milestones children experience growing up are affected by what's happening in their life during those milestones. A child establishes safety and confidence in their first year of life. During these months, they begin to associate that their caretakers are there for them and provide an immediate response. If they're hungry, they're fed. If they're wet, their diaper is changed, conveying to the infant that their basic needs are not only addressed but satisfied.

"A divorce at this age can impact the child greatly," Collom says. "Their needs aren't being met due to emotional distress. Kids are resilient. They live through many, many, crises, but it does have an effect. That's the thing; it does have an effect."

Custody

Over a year after the proceedings began, the courts ruled in favor of Kay. Though she won full custody, Kay was generous with her ex-husband, allowing Ronnie weekly visitation with his daughter as well as having her every other weekend.

"I didn't think about my situation. I just thought about my daughter," Kay says. "I didn't want to damage her any more than she may have been."

Kay's attitude toward her daughter's welfare is right on par with what the experts recommend.

"[Parents] have to be adult enough to say, 'We're not going to let this dispute interfere with our children. I'm not going to alienate. I'm going to support your relationship with these children,'" Minerva says.

Kay deserves a lot of credit. Putting aside personal feelings is not an acceptable option for many divorced couples, but it should be. "It's not about you. It's about the child and what's in the best interest of the child," Shannon, adds.

"As parents, we have to tuck aside our emotions. Continue to foster and build the self-esteem of the child and help them weather this so that the divorce is minimally traumatizing to them," Shannon says.

Difficult Decisions

Kay was faced with one of the most difficult eventualities that many times follows a divorce: Michelle's visitation with her father now included visits with "the other woman."

Kay's stomach churned as she unbuckled Michelle from her car seat. She reached for her daughter's backpack filled with clothes, snacks, and her favorite book, *Goodnight Moon*.

"Ready to see Daddy," Kay asked through gritted teeth.

"Dada," Michelle said, giggling and smiling as her mother lifted her from the car and hoisted the backpack onto her shoulder.

Kay clutched her daughter to her chest as she walked the short path to Tess's front door.

"Mama squeeze too hard," Michelle said.

Kay released the vice grip she had on her daughter and rang the doorbell. Moments later, Tess appeared, her arms reaching out for Michelle.

"Come on, sweetie. Come to Tessie," she said.

Kay sidestepped Tess, keeping Michelle from her as she entered the house and then dropped the backpack to the floor.

"Where's Ronnie," she asked, looking left and right.

"We needed some groceries, so he offered to go to the store," Tess said, "He's just so thoughtful."

Kay laughed out loud, making no effort to censor her response. She set Michelle down on the floor, fished through the backpack, and pulled out a stuffed bear.

"Here, sweetie, play with Max," Kay said.

The two women looked everywhere but at each other while Michelle played on the floor.

"Would you like some juice, sweetie?" Tess said as she turned and headed to the kitchen.

Michelle dropped her bear and followed after her, clapping her hands, calling out, "Tessie, Tessie!"

"You can see yourself out, Kay. I gotta run," Tess said over her shoulder. "Michelle needs me."

Trust and Transitioning

Kay also struggled with Ronnie's role in their daughter's life. Who was this man that she'd married? If he was the kind of man who could abandon her and his infant daughter, had she ever really known him?

"In the beginning, I didn't trust any of his judgments. I didn't know who he was. I didn't know how he would be with our child at first. It was very scary," Kay says, shaking her head.

Ronnie broke it off with Tess soon after their son Trevor was born, and with her departure, Kay was offered the opportunity to rebuild her trust in Ronnie. But even after the tension between her parents abated, Michelle was still transitioning from one home to the other, which is all too common for children of divorce. This transitioning has the potential to create a great deal of emotional angst and anxiety. Many times a child's only release from those feelings is to act out. Kay experienced that with Michelle.

"I want my cookie! I want it now," Michelle said, tears streaming down her cheeks and her face red and puffy.

Kay stared at her child, who just moments ago was smiling and happily waving goodbye to her father as he headed out the front door.

"Michelle, it's almost time for supper," Kay said in a soothing tone. "You can have a cookie after dinner if you're a good girl. Okay?"

The three-year-old's tears subsided as she stared up at her mother. Then she placed both hands on her hips.

"Daddy gives me cookies," she said. "I want to go to his house."

Kay turned away from her daughter. Now it was her turn to cry.

"I don't know if it was because of the different parenting styles, or like she has to get back into Mom's parenting mode, because Dad is very different, but she would return home with a sort of a chip on her shoulder," Kay says.

In this type of location-based transition, the experts agree that a good way to help ease a child's anxiety is to allow them to be more receptive to the new environment. Shannon suggests a good place to start is allowing the child to set up their room at the new home.

"It's important that the kids have pictures of Mom and Dad and the family unit at each household," Shannon says.

Collom suggests letting the child pick out their bed and furnishings as a way to help them feel they have a say in the situation. Minerva adds, it's important to allow the child to bring items from the old place to the new one. Familiar items provide comfort and stability.

"So there's a sense of continuity. Everything isn't disruptive. It's a way for them to have a voice about something in their world," Shannon says.

Masking True Feelings

Over the years, Kay noticed aspects of her daughter's behavior she considered unusual for a child her age.

"She's very responsible. I feel that is part of her. She's very on top of it," Kay says. "I don't think kids her age even have to think about that if they're not from a divorced family. She's a perfectionist, and she wants things to be a certain way. She wants to be in control of her stuff. I think because her life is so, you're here one day, and you're there that day, she needs to know her schedule.

"She's very aware and considerate when it comes to other people and their feelings. Even with her dad and I, she doesn't ever want to hurt our feelings by saying, 'I want to go to his house today, or I want to do something with Mom.'"

According to Collom, many children tend to "mask or cover up their true feelings" to hide the fear of abandonment that the majority of children of divorce experience.

"One of the biggest things that people don't realize is what a child sees, no matter what age, even as an adult, is really what I call abandonment," Collom says. "If you can leave Mom, and Mom can leave you, you can leave me, and so they run for cover. They run to protect themselves. So, they begin to cover up because, in their head, they're saying I can be left too."

This unconscious fear may explain Michelle's unconditional acceptance of the drastic changes in her life, beginning with her father's departure. As those changes transpired, Michelle's demeanor continued to be one of acceptance and happiness.

Only Child

Less than a year after her parents divorced, her half-brother Trevor entered the family. The children developed a strong bond and saw each other nearly every day as they both attended the same school. In addition to the growing affection Michelle had for Trevor, her curiosity regarding his role in the family continued to grow.

In addition to Trevor, Michelle welcomed Greg, Kay's second husband, into the family. Her mother's remarriage produced additional half-siblings for Michelle, as Kay and Greg have two daughters, now three and five years old. Michelle continues to embrace her role as big sister to all three siblings and, according to Kay, plays the role of "momma bear" to them all.

In another sense, however, Michelle is an only child, and experts agree that only children tend to exhibit an unusually strong sense of concern regarding their parents' welfare, especially in the case of divorce.

"I think when there is an only child, there is a kind of greater sense of responsibility for the well-being of the parent," Minerva says.

This explains Michelle's positive reaction to her father's remarriage, which took place a few years ago.

"When her dad wasn't married, I think she felt like she had to take care of him and be with him, or she'd feel guilty," Kay explains.

Does Michelle's status of "only child" play into her willingness to please, or is it the result of being a child of divorce? Either way, it's obvious that at this stage in her life, she appears to exhibit the behavior of a normal ten-year-old little girl in both households.

"So, I think what's good is that she has a good family unit over there with her brother, and they have a good time," Kay says. "And she's here, and she has her sisters and all that. She seems happy with both houses."

Experts agree children of divorce have the same ability to achieve equal levels of stability and happiness in their lives. The determining factor of how that plays out is a responsibility that falls squarely on the shoulders of the parents and their behavior toward not only the child but to each other.

The Time for Honesty

Kay and Ronnie have made great efforts to secure their daughter's happiness, but the future holds a great deal more for them all. The revelation of why her parents divorced is yet to be disclosed to Michelle, but it is an eventuality and elicits a level of concern beyond the scope of parenting.

Ten years after the normal divorce, Kay and Ronnie's decision to end their marriage continues to affect their daughter. This fact is substantiated by Michelle's propensity to continually search for answers to questions that have never been fully addressed.

Recently, Michelle jumped out of Ronnie's car, giving her father a cursory wave, and headed to the front door where Kay stood waiting for her.

"Did you have fun at your dad's?" Kay asked as Michelle dropped her backpack to the floor.

"Yeah, Mom, we had a picnic on Saturday, and today we went to the park," Michelle said, then added, "Dad's a lot of fun. Why didn't you stay together? What happened? Do you love Dad?" Michelle said.

"I answer the questions that I feel she can understand," Kay says. Although her concern is growing that the day is fast approaching when she can no longer avoid telling Michelle the truth.

No matter how ugly the truth, the experts agree that parents should try to present the facts to a child with a level of positivity. Minerva proposes that when dealing with the subject of infidelity, parents try to be general and non-specific when explaining to the child why the couple divorced.

"Taking out your anger at the ex-spouse through the child can only harm the child," Minerva cautions.

Kay readily admits it's something she and Ronnie need to figure out.

"I don't know how we'll go about doing it. I've been thinking about that since she was ten months old," Kay says. "Ronnie told me he's going to be honest with her when that time comes and tell her the truth. We'll see.

I think if I was her, and I found out what my dad did to her and me, I think it would affect my relationship with my dad, definitely, and myself too. There'd be a lot of internal anger. I think that it's going to affect her when she gets to that age where she understands the situation."

Ultimately, Kay's hope is for Michelle to remain the happy and well-adjusted child she is today, even after she has a better understanding of what transpired between her parents.

"If you met her, I don't think you'd ever know that she came from a divorced family," Kay says. "She's content. She's happy with herself. She's happy with her family. She's just a very positive kid, and she's always been that way. She's such a good kid and has a good head on her shoulders. I'm hoping she makes good choices and talks to us about everything the way that she has been."

Michelle's reaction to the truth is yet to be known. But one certainty in this family is that Kay and Ronnie will always put their daughter's welfare first. Along the way, if they discover that she, or they, need additional support, they won't hesitate to reach out for help.

My Thoughts

Michelle's story is ultimately one of unconditional love. The fact that her parents were able to sidestep their anger and negativity toward one another for the sake of their child, throughout the divorce and after, is an example for all parents to follow.

I'd like to say I handled my divorce as well, but I can't. What I can say is that my top priority was my son, who was ten at the time. The need to remove him from an abusive home propelled me to initiate the divorce. But with the proceedings underway, I found the certainty I felt began to waver.

That uncertainty was fueled by fear—fear of the unknown, fear of my inability to provide for my son, and fear for myself. How could I put us in jeopardy like this? But as the pendulum swung back to reality, bringing with it the memories of my husband's explosive torrents of rage that led to my cowering in the dark corner of our bedroom in the late-night hours praying for help, the certainty would once again return. My assurance that leaving that world behind—even if I had no idea what our new world would be—was best for my son.

As concerned as I was for him, the rollercoaster ride of emotions I experienced resulted in—more times than I care to admit—the transformation of the mom he'd always known into a woman battling her own insecurities while trying to maintain a sense of normalcy. In other words, a complete stranger.

My son's reaction to this confusing transformation amidst all the other countless changes taking place in his life was difficult to decipher, mostly because I was too afraid to examine them. I chose instead to ignore his silences, which were at times, followed by outbursts of anger. The result was that when my son needed me most, I'd failed him.

I can't undo my past mistakes, but if I could go back in time, my priority would be to realize that the first year after the divorce was not only my most difficult year but my son's most difficult year as well. I kept forgetting this fact, as so many divorced parents do.

Despite my countless failings, I was awarded a priceless gift. Right around the one-year anniversary of the divorce, my son and I sat on his bed and had a long, frank conversation. I tried to be as honest as I could regarding all that had happened and how it made me feel and why I felt there was no other choice. At the end of the talk, exhausted by my admissions and ready to head to bed, he turned to me and said, "You made the right choice, Mom."

The elation I experienced at that moment filled me with a renewed energy, not only that night but for the weeks and months to follow. Even though the new normal was nothing like the old, it was a normal both of us had begun to accept—and even enjoy. The journey we traveled was grueling, but I have absolutely no doubt that it was necessary. It's that certainty that kept us moving forward, and it's that certainty that continues to bond us. I believe it always will. ❤

THE EXPERTS WEIGH IN

1 How does divorce affect children at different ages?

Minerva: We know that in those first few years, zero to three, a sudden abandonment is potentially devastating to the development of the child's psyche. It does not matter that they don't have language. In fact, [not having] language means that it is recorded sensorily. But as children get older, there is more understanding of the emotional pain and disruption to the parents.

Shannon: When children get older, a lot of kids do have a hard time when their parents get a divorce. To them, the fighting wasn't that bad, or the arguing wasn't that bad. Kids, as with any individual when they have a trauma in their life—[it's] a trauma that Mom and Dad are getting divorced—will go through the phases of death and dying, the grief phase. It's a loss. It's the loss of the family unit.

Scott: There is research that small children, even before they have verbal skills, do pick up on the energy in the house. I would say it's definitely more detrimental for younger children simply because they don't have the skills to process or talk about it, and it becomes so much more internalized.

Older children, teenagers, and adolescents have developed enough to develop coping skills for themselves. It's still detrimental, but they've developed further along. Not to say that [young] children aren't resilient.

Terranova: For a child with parents that break up before they're aware of a big, dynamic shift, perhaps if they're under say age two or three, the child might be less confused by this since the parents don't live together. When divorce happens early on, there is a level of acceptance that things are going to be different versus the situations when the child is a little older and used to a certain routine. In that case, it would certainly be odd if the parents weren't together.

Collom: You want to look at the milestones in the child's life. Zero to one is the time a child establishes safety and confidence, trust vs. mistrust, that the loved ones will be there for them, and that their needs will be met. The response by the loved ones is immediate. Divorce at this age can impact the child greatly. Their needs aren't being met due to emotional distress. They will immediately regress, having accidents. Once past that age, they regress in their emotional development because of the impact [of the divorce]. It's a coping mechanism. They're trying to go to a time that was safe and comfortable, when things were okay, so they're regressing emotionally, and it's not intellectual. It's all psychological.

One of the biggest things that people don't realize is what a child sees, no matter what age, even as an adult. If you can leave Mom and Mom can leave you, I can be left too. So they run for cover. They run to protect themselves.

2 What is the best way for parents to explain to a child that Mom and Dad are getting a divorce?

Minerva: They have to be adult enough to say we're not going to let this dispute interfere with our children. I'm not going to alienate; I'm going to support [the other parent's] relationship with these children. So that is the best preparation that they can do. In terms of how they present that to children, again, keep any kind of conflict out of their direct observation. Keep the kids out of it. Keep it clean; don't fight dirty.

Collom: Two adults united is always best to help them with the transition. You try to include that child and get them off the hook of it having anything to do with them. Hopefully, you have two healthy enough parents that can approach it in a way that's supportive toward the child.

Marsh: Sensitive children may be affected more so than a child who is less sensitive, which should be considered from the announcement, through the entire process of the divorce. So consider the personality of the child.

Terranova: The more parents are communicating or allowing the child to process things in a healthier manner, the more they're given permission to feel their feelings, talk about their feelings, verbalize sadness or anger, or even rage without being shut down, the healthier the atmosphere is for people to really show up and process and work through their feelings, I'm finding kids go through it and have fewer of those feelings of being left or abandoned.

3 What impact does parental alienation have on a child?

Minerva: Parental alienation is where one parent lies to the child about the other parent or undermines the child's relationship to the other parent. They are playing really dirty pool. It makes the child feel like one parent is bad, and one parent is good. Or they have to decide who is good and who is bad.

Collom: Many parents have a lot of bickering and fighting using the child as a pawn in the continued anger and resentment they have for each other, and that makes it worse for the child. Sometimes the child figures out the game and decides they want to get something out of the situation, and they tell the parent they live with they want to live with the other parent, a sort of manipulation of the situation. Although, in some cases, there is a genuine connection with the other parent.

Shannon: What I say to parents is you are forever connected [to your co-parent] because of your child. If the parents continue to exist in conflict after the divorce, it can have a horrible impact on children. I think parents need to be aware that their children will do as well as [the parents] will do. It's super important for the emotional wellbeing of the child that there be neutrality.

Marsh: Co-parenting means any parents that are no longer in a union are parenting this child or children, and they're operating on the same values, the same love for the children, and concern for their well-being, now and long term. They can share their goals on how to raise the child; that's the perfect scenario.

Blaming the other parent is so destructive. The child is wondering if there is something wrong with them because they love the other parent. You don't vent to your kid about the other parent, so find somebody else. I think it's really damaging in terms of setting that child up for all kinds of problems, [such as] interpersonal problems in relationships [for] the rest of their lives. Do they become somebody who is a people pleaser? Do they become very co-dependent?

Scott: It's hard for a parent to separate out their role in their relationship as husband and wife and their role as a parent. No matter how bad it is, maintain some sort of distance for the child's sake; it's really important. Divorce is incredibly stressful and difficult, and there's a lot of unresolved issues that come to the surface, and we know the raw spots in our partners. When we are no longer entrusted in that relationship, when that's ended, sometimes it's like all bets are off, and everything that's been unresolved comes out in a very negative way.

Terranova: Using a child for their own emotional needs is very dangerous for anyone, and most importantly, for a child that's trying to understand their world that's been broken. Learning how badly one parent was treated by the other is difficult for the child to hear and could cause a divide in regard to their feelings toward the one parent.

4 How beneficial is professional therapy for a child of divorce?

Minerva: Clearly, not every kid who goes through a divorce gets that. I can't say I would absolutely say yes, you have to, unless there are some behaviors or situations that can push the tipping point. So, you, [the parent], can do some of the active listening where you can say, "It seems like you're feeling really sad. You really miss Dad right now, right?" Or, "You're really mad. Let's go play some basketball for a while." Have some physical releases that help them to express those things in one way or another.

Collom: You don't force them. Sometimes they don't even know how they feel. The parent can go to therapy.

Scott: Every child doesn't need to be in therapy if they're going through a divorce. They may not be in a place where they even want to process it. They may not want to understand it. Sometimes you have to wait and ask the child. Be there [for the child] as a resource. Help them understand what they're experiencing, and separate that out from however you're feeling as a parent.

Think about a car on the road—you hit enough pot holes, and your car is out of alignment. My job is to simply help somebody get back aligned with who they are. Things like divorce, moving, death of a loved one, job change, all of those things are huge potholes. They shake us up, they shake us at our foundation, and we have to figure out how to get aligned.

Marsh: In my experience with working with children who've experienced losing a parent, many times, a child is encouraged to be strong and keep their feelings to themselves. The same can happen in situations of divorce, so having an impartial therapist would be very helpful for the child and provide them a safe place to share their feelings.

5 How long after the divorce should a parent wait before introducing a new partner?

Minerva: I would wait until you know that [the relationship] is something that has a future expectation. I don't think they should just be introduced when they become the stepparent. There should be some transition in the beginning. I think there is a risk for sexual abuse when bringing unknown people into the home. The guestimate is one in three girls and one in four or five boys have been sexually abused. And if there is a rotating household of strangers coming into the house without there being a lot of discernment before you bring that person in, it just seems like an excessive risk.

Marsh: If either or both parents get into another relationship where you're bringing in another parental figure, first make sure to have really clear communication boundaries intact and ensure that they are functioning well. The child must be thinking or feeling on some level, "I can see my parent really likes you or loves you, and I don't know how I feel about that." All the [parents] want, especially the biological parent, is nothing more than for everyone to be a big happy family, and [they] may often be in denial when it isn't.

Terranova: They're going to be looking at the world around them to decide if it's safe or not, and so if they're trusting of their parents, then, of course, they're going to be weighing that in the context when they meet this new person. And, of course, there are the variables of how a person is introduced, how quickly and how much of an opportunity the child's had to get to know this person before they're involved in parenting or trying to help out in the home. Some children are very extroverted and kind of gravitate toward social relationships and interactions and may be more inclined. While others may warm up very slowly and be more methodical, thoughtful, and more introverted, and that child may need more time to bring someone new into their life.

6 What are the challenges faced by stepfamilies?

Marsh: Often, the younger [the child is], the more receptive they are regarding a stepparent. As they get older, definitely not so much. Have a good understanding and assessment of where your child is with the breakup in the first place. If they're still grieving, help them process the feelings around this loss because it really is very much a loss. So, wherever they are, the children, in their coming through it, they need to be allowed to have that time before they can be expected to be accepting. A lot is expected of kids of divorce.

You had one household, and now you have two. There's still going to be the perception that all things could not be equal any longer because it's two separate households now. And this is even with divorced families that end up with fifty-fifty custody. Newly blended, they don't blend, especially the older ones. For that pre-adolescent and adolescent, their trajectory is out of the family anyway. Their newly chosen families are their friends, their peers. It can be very hard and very complex. I think for stepfamilies, with the understanding that their new family is born of loss, they can certainly, with patience and a sense of humor and their own self-care, understand that they can become a cohesive family, with their own new traditions, and create their own memories. It's probably not going to look like what their first one did.

Scott: Everyone has different parenting styles. When you slam two different families together they're going to do just the opposite. And when there's no emotional conversation, there's no emotional connection. When those families come together, it would be great to do family therapy. I think sometimes people get together and blend their families, and then they realize they have two totally different styles, and it's chaos.

Terranova: If the child is expected to just jump in and accept it, [half-siblings], it could have a damaging effect. I think it would be very important that the home environment is considerate of the level at which a child can process the information and speak at that level. [You're] not speaking down but speaking openly and honestly at an educationally, developmentally appropriate level when a baby is to be introduced into the circle as well.

The bonding process and how the family handles that is crucial in regard to detachment issues. If the parent expects acceptance of the new child or stepchild without allowing their child to express their true feelings, those kinds of authoritarian methods are not only damaging in any situation but especially so when a child is confused about where they belong.

How healthy was the divorce? Are these two individuals able to co-parent and then agree on how things are going to go down, and if the co-parenting is solid the likelihood of a new parent coming in there may be a more positive fit because there's a good healthy communication going on. Identifying the role of the stepparent is important for the primary parent to clarify for both the child's sake and the sake of their new partner.

7 What is the best way to handle holidays post-divorce?

Minerva: It helps to have a plan. I am a big fan of flexibility. As much as possible, be supportive and accommodating, while also staying flexible.

Collom: There's what I call an emotional tug of war inside [the child] already as those things come up because they're used to tradition. They're used to things being a certain way. So, you [should] really try and help them by preparing ahead of time—this is how it's going to be. They're going to have emotions about that. They're going to have feelings about that. They may or may not be able to verbalize that. That's where play will help verbalize it. Preparing and talking about it. "What's that like for you?" It's okay to say, "What would you like?" But that doesn't mean you do it. You're just getting them to share a little more—affirmation, rather than trying to fix it.

Shannon: With the holidays, it can be an exciting yet traumatizing time of year for kids depending upon again the traditions and the extended family. When parents can have their routines at their house and have flexibility with the kids, the kids will do best. Some families alternate holidays. Putting a positive spin on it, you get two Christmases.

8 How can parents help a child transition to living in two houses?

Minerva: Where possible, be able to let them buy in with that and have some choices about that. I think it helps them feel like there is a little bit of an adventure that happens. I also think it's important to have some items they can transition from the old place to the new place so that there's a sense of continuity; everything isn't disruptive. It's a way for them to have a voice about something in their world. They didn't get to choose this divorce. They didn't have a vote in that situation. But to be able to say, "I like this," or "I don't like that," [giving children] something that they have control over in that environment helps them not feel quite so powerless.

Collom: In those situations, you want the child's input. "What kind of bed do you want?" Include the child in the new home, like picking their own bed and furnishings.

Shannon: It's important that the kids have pictures of Mom and Dad and the family unit at each new household. It's not about you, it's about the child and what's in the best interest of the child, so we always look at the best interest of the child. Foster and build the self-esteem of the child and help them weather this so that the divorce their parents go through is minimally traumatizing to them. It's going to have an impact. There's negativity there, but it can be, "Okay, Mom and Dad are better apart."

Terranova: It's really dependent on the quality of the divorce. Some families still do family holidays together or vacations together. For those families that break up and there is no more family home, it will have a larger impact on [those children] than the family that is able to stay congenial after the divorce.

9 Why does a child act out, and what is the best way to respond?

Collom: Most of the time a child will start to act out, which is normal for crises and divorce. They regress. They act out more. Extroverts become introverts, and introverts become more extroverted. Those are signs that they're under a lot of anxiety, a lot of stress. They get aggressive with their toys—two dolls fighting, cars crashing. They play it out through those things. Children use matches and fire because that's anger, and fire is a reflection of being angry inside, burning inside, and wanting to destroy things. What the child is really asking for is some kind of connection.

Scott: Acting out doesn't mean that they're aggressive outwardly. Acting out may mean they close off and shut down. They may protect themselves by disassociating and not be present. That's what I hear, especially from the teens.

Terranova: First and foremost, just to be able to say this is tough and we're in it, and we're present with it, and we're acknowledging that it's hard, I would say is a fundamental piece of this. One of my key phrases that I often use with parents is to tell them to tell their own child, "This is a really tough time. I really am feeling these feelings, but I've got this. Don't worry. You don't have to fix this." That's a key factor.

How do you address past abuse with a child of divorce?

Marsh: I think it's very harmful to them. It's no secret that for healthy child development, children need stability, and they really need stability from their parents. If there's antagonism between the parents—actually fighting in the presence of children that becomes physical, it's seen in the eyes of the law as detrimental for the child in their mental and emotional development.

Shannon: What I've seen in my own work, depending upon the severity of the abuse, depends on how well the child will do, and then early intervention. ❤

Additional Help

Terranova: I've not seen any positive outcome of families staying together for the sake of the kids. If you can model two solid, healthy homes, it's far superior to one dysfunctional home.

Scott: Sometimes a child may go through a really horrible divorce, but they may have a lot of support. They may have a lot of internal coping mechanisms and may go through it easier than somebody else who has a different temperament, less coping skills, less support.

Any time a parent can own their own mistakes in the process of divorce with the children, then there can be healing done there. When we talk about what is best for kids going through divorce, I think it's really important to talk about owning it to a child. Being like, "You know I didn't do such a great job when your dad and I were going through the divorce, and I said some really bad things about him, and I know that impacted you, and I'm really sorry about that. It's a huge thing, and it can be difficult." We absorb whatever happens in our family. It becomes a part of us. So, you can be divorced, and it can be a miserable divorce, and it could be a miserable marriage, and the kids are still going to have that be part of them. We can still recover and heal from it. It is a process. I think that's the thing that's really important to let people know.

Parents going through a divorce, if they're not doing what they need to, taking care of themselves, they have less to give to their children. As long as you're talking to your child, and as long as there is love, and as long as you're expressing and being emotionally connected to the child, the factors around [aren't] important. I think as human beings, you have a right to be in a relationship that is the kind of relationship you want, and that's a beautiful thing to share and for your child to actually see.

Marsh: Parentification of the child, where the child is expected to be the emotional partner of the parent. You're really doing a disservice to your kid, and you don't even realize that you're doing it. That's still an inappropriate expectation that you're placing on the kid.

Shannon: I think it's really important that parents do not talk about the divorce around the children, and they are not to see court documents.

Collom: What parents need to do is to be observant, watch your child, and their actions. See what their play is about. See what's happening in school—if they have a sudden regression in grades or throw themselves into their schoolwork. ❤

References

Pete Collom, interview by author, November 16, 2016

Kimberly Shannon, interview by author, November 18, 2016

Vicki Minerva, interview by author, April 18, 2017

Dr. David Royko, interview by author, January 13, 2018

Linnea Terranova, interview by author, January 23, 2019

Eleanor Scott, interview by author, February 1, 2019

Jayne Marsh, interview by author, February 19, 2019

Australian Institute of Family Studies, journal data base—Gilroy Library, January 9, 2020

Kathleen Coulborn Faller, University of Arkansas at Little Rock Law Review, volume 22 issue 3

ABOUT THE AUTHOR

Kimberly Ewertz has been a reporter for more than three decades. She began her journalism career as an editor at St. Louis Community College Meramec. During her time there, she won two Missouri College Media Association Awards.

After college, she wrote for numerous publications throughout the years, including the *Webster Groves Times*, the *Gilroy Dispatch*, *gmhToday Magazine*, the *Morgan Hill Times*, *Palo Alto Weekly*, *Redwood City Patch*, and the *Los Altos Town Crier*.

In her extensive work in journalism, Ewertz has focused on feature articles and delights in highlighting people and their accomplishments.

After twelve years of marriage, in 1990, Ewertz filed for divorce, propelling her and her then ten-year-old son into a journey of irrevocable change. That journey is the impetus for this book. Her message to all parents and children navigating the uncharted waters of post-divorce is one of hope: the road will be long, it will be difficult, but in the end, it will be worth it.

Ewertz and her husband, Steve, and their dogs, Murphy and Charlie, reside in the small town of Gilroy. ♥

CPSIA information can be obtained
at www.ICGtesting.com
Printed in the USA
FSHW020023231020

9 781942 586883